Healthy Clergy
Wounded Healers

ROBERTA CHAPIN WALMSLEY
ADAIR T. LUMMIS

Healthy Clergy
Wounded Healers
Their Families and
Their Ministries

Church Publishing Incorporated, New York

Copyright © 1997 by Roberta Chapin Walmsley and Adair T. Lummis.

Library of Congress Cataloging-in-Publication Data

Walmsley, Roberta Chapin, 1933–

    Healthy clergy, wounded healers / by Roberta Chapin Walmsley,
Adair T. Lummis.

    p. cm.

    Includes bibliographical references.

    ISBN 0-89869-253-9 (pbk.)

    1. Episcopal Church—Clergy—Health and hygiene. 2. Episcopal Church—
Clergy—Mental health. 3. Episcopal Church—Clergy—Family relationships.
4. Anglican Communion—United States—Clergy.
I. Lummis, Adair T. II. Title.

BX5965.W35 1997   97–19085

262'. 14373—dc21   CIP

Church Pubishing Incorporated
445 Fifth Avenue
New York NY 10016

5 4 3 2 1

This book is dedicated to
Mrs. Christine Folwell,
without whose creativity and leadership
the Episcopal Clergy Family Project
research would never have been initiated.
She continues to be much involved in the project
as a major consultant and advisor.

Contents

Foreword

This book is about clergymen and clergywomen and their families. It is the result of a program begun in 1986 by the Episcopal Family Network to help clergy and spouses be healthy and stay healthy. That program, the Clergy Family Project, continues to this day. Its focus has been on creating a profile of the healthy priest and spouse, identifying attributes and behaviors that contribute to their health, and helping dioceses institute programs, policies, and resources that preserve their health. The Clergy Family Project is not just for married clergy. By the inclusion of the word *family* in the title of the program, we recognize the changing face of families in our culture today, the fact that no one is without some family connection, and that most people have a social system which sustains them.

The Episcopal Family Network is an agency affiliated with the national offices of the Episcopal Church. EFN was established as the result of a resolution passed at the 1979 General Convention which stated that the church needed to give greater attention to serving *all* families. The Clergy Family Project is one response instituted by EFN. Given the close relationship between clergy and the parish, the Episcopal Family Network concluded that one way to begin addressing the issues of all families would be to focus on clergy and their families. The theory supporting this choice is that healthy clergy, in their particular leadership roles in congregations, help to beget healthy congregations and a healthy church.

Twenty-three dioceses have participated in the Clergy Family Project since 1986. When a diocese takes part in the project, it engages in a three-part process. The first stage involves a committee which represents the clergy families in the diocese in a process of building community and developing a vision. The second stage includes the distribution of a twenty-four-page questionnaire to clergy and spouses in the diocese and the interpretation of the data the questionnaire generates. The third stage involves the diocese in the development of actions which are responsive to the data.

The response to the questionnaire has been excellent in each diocese, well over 50 percent, particularly among parochial clergy. Approximately 2,000 clergy and 1,300 spouses have responded to the questionnaire. *Episcopal Clergy Families in the Eighties*, a report of the results in the first six dioceses that participated in the project, was published in 1988.* The analysis in this book is based primarily on data gathered from 907 clergy and 572 spouses in twelve dioceses that participated in the project between 1990–1993.** The conclusions reached from the present data are not significantly different from those drawn in the earlier analysis.

The stories from which the illustrations in this book are taken

---

*The information cited in the 1988 report is from the Dioceses of Alabama, Central Florida, Tennessee, Connecticut, Maryland, and Massachusetts.
**The Dioceses of Atlanta, Central New York, Hawaii, Iowa, Kansas, Kentucky, Lexington, Missouri, Northern Indiana, Oregon, Southern Ohio, and Western North Carolina.

come from a population that is largely male and white. The project tries scrupulously to assure that confidentiality is maintained. Thus, in order that no one is identified or feels identified, most of the stories are taken from the majority. We have found, however, that what is required for a healthy life crosses all categories of people, though each group may have issues that are particularly relevant to it.

This book is for clergy, spouses of clergy, and lay people—and, of course, bishops, their spouses and others involved with clergy and their families. Clergy often say that they wish lay people knew what life is like for them. We hope that this book helps give them a voice. Indeed, how a parish treats its clergy and their families and what it understands about their needs and circumstances also contribute to healthy congregational life. At the end of the book we have included a series of questions related to the discussion in each chapter. We would urge their use in a variety of ways—for individual reflection, as couples, with peer groups, in clergy and lay discussion groups, and other configurations that would benefit from such a discussion.

One objective of the Clergy Family Project is to put data into action. This book is one example of that. It is the collaborative effort of a social worker who is also a writer and a sociologist who is also a research analyst. Together we have tried to turn the language of analysis into a narrative that speaks to the lives of clergy and their families. At the same time, for those who want to know on what we base what we say, we have included the significant tables and charts.

We are grateful to the recent presidents of the Episcopal Family Network, Bishop William J. Winterrowd and Mrs. Anne Lea Tuohy, for their oversight of this action-research project and the vision they have demonstrated. We also value the skill and hard work of the Clergy Family Project consultants—Ran Chase, Julie Coffey, Beth Coleman, Christine Folwell, Nancy Hopkins, and Jan McDonald—who helped the participating dioceses understand and use their survey data in meeting the needs of their clergy families. The consultants have played an essential role in the design of this project. They have also contributed their insights to the interpretation of the survey results, and have provided valuable suggestions of ways in which dioceses might improve the overall health of clergy families. We are grateful to Mary Jane Ross whose considerable secretarial skills have been invaluable to the Clergy Family Project. Of course, we cannot forget all the clergy and spouses who participated in the project and provided the data on which this study is based. We deeply appreciate their trust and willingness to give of their time.

It takes money to run a program. Each participating diocese incurred expenses in its participation in the project and development of resources for clergy families. In addition, The Episcopal Family Network and the Clergy Family Project are indebted to the Church Pension Group, Trinity Church (NYC), the Episcopal Church Foundation, the Episcopal Church Center, and individuals, including especially our Presiding Bishop, Edmond Browning, for their support of the project.

Finally, the data analysis and writing of this book could not have been undertaken without a grant from the Trinity Church Grants Program to Hartford Seminary, the repository of data collected from clergy and spouses in all participating dioceses. Mrs. Odessa Elliott, their Special Projects Associate, has unofficially served as a research consultant to this project, pinpointing emerging themes and posing important questions that this research can address.

Roberta Chapin Walmsley
Adair T. Lummis
February 1997

CHAPTER I

Health and Wholeness: The Challenge

If I had it to do over again, would I? I'm not so sure. Times seemed simpler when I started out thirty-five years ago. The church is becoming increasingly complex—meaning, the complexity of the expectations placed on clergy by the congregation, the world, the diocese. There is more administration, more meetings, a lot of organizational maintenance just to keep afloat. From my perspective, I am looking at declining resources—people and money. Put all that together and they are real dangers to clergy and to their families.

George was ordained a priest in the Episcopal Church in 1958. The "fifties," as he remembers them, was a decade in which churches boomed. George went straight through college and seminary and into a curacy in a large parish. He was excited about the life he had chosen and the prospects for ministry that ordination opened for him. Following his two-year curacy, George became the rector of a medium-size suburban parish. Twenty years ago he accepted a call to a parish in the heart of a small city which lies within a very large and sprawling metropolitan "mega-region." Historically, the parish has carried on a lively ministry to the city. In recent years, however, it has struggled to stay alive in an economically troubled area. Many people key to the life and work of the parish in the seventies have died or retired to a warmer climate. Many of the people who have replaced them don't stay very long. In fact, to those who stay, the turnover of parishioners seems constant. Moreover, the newcomers pledge less than members of previous generations. Their schedules are also so tight that they have little time to spare to help with the ongoing ministry of the parish. The numbers to do that are shrinking, as George says.

George's observation about the events of the past thirty-five years is that the boom of the fifties has been followed by a time of change in the church and in the culture so swift that it defies almost anybody's adaptive capacity. Many days he is very discouraged about what has happened to the vocation to which he so eagerly leapt as a young man. He is counting the days to retirement. George's ambivalence about his ministry and his anxiety over declining resources is likely to be echoed by other priests and pastors across the mainline denominations. Changes that take place within a culture affect and challenge the personal and professional lives of clergy, as well as the existence of the religious institutions of which they are a part. The distress and uncertainty arising out of rapid and demanding change can also intensify the feelings that accompany the expectations that clergy, their families, church executives, and laity have about what clergy ought to "be like" and "do."

The Ordained Ministry—Myth and Reality

While George struggles to manage the increasing complexities of his vocation, he also has a nagging sense that society does not view his profession with the esteem it did thirty-five years ago. Yet, he feels that clergy are still expected, even by the unchurched, to be models of stability and moral behavior. The failure of clergy to meet this expectation is newsworthy. "Priest Guilty of Sexual Misconduct" has become a blazing headline for the nineties. Church and popular publications feature articles on clergy who opt out of parish ministry, or the ordained ministry entirely, to escape the stress and tension which sap their energy and seem to turn their calling to ashes. Congregations and judicatories are absorbed in interventions which become essential when clergy are accused of inappropriate sexual behavior or abuse of drugs and alcohol. The divorce rate in clergy families, although about equal to that of the rest of the population, symbolizes for some the breakdown of the church and the failure of clergy to set an example of commitment. Such slippage from the pedestal of propriety is faith-shaking for some; others view it as yet another example of the church as an institution which attracts emotionally vulnerable people to its ordained ranks.[1] All this has an impact on George and adds to his present state of dissatisfaction.

Dysfunctional behavior in clergy makes news. Misconduct and burnout are clearly problems which demand the church's response. Yet, when dysfunction commands the major portion of what the public hears and reads about clergy, the unrealistic image of "the pastor" already held by many, lay and ordained, may be distorted even further. Despite the many changes that have taken place in the church and culture in the latter days of the twentieth century, a common image that the word "minister" still often evokes is of a wholesome, devoted, attentive man. He is a preacher, teacher, counselor and visionary who draws people to the church. Much like Superman, he is a multi-talented person who can "leap tall buildings." The woman to whom he is married is hospitable, devoted, and supportive. Her life focuses on *his* ministry. The picture is complete with the addition of at least two children. Yet, like the dysfunctional cleric at the other end of the continuum, the "ideal" priest is but a fragment of the total picture of who and what a priest is.

Emory University historian E. Brooks Holifield suggests that the image commonly associated with a priest or minister is based on the cultural "heroes" of an era. Heroes *can* leap tall buildings. Although the image may change with the times,[2] the effect of being perceived as any type of cultural hero makes living an ordinary life difficult for most people. Clergy are no exception. Lay people may think the images reflect the way clergy are—or certainly should be. Clergy often emotionally buy into the images and feel they are the ones they should mirror—or certainly *appear* to mirror. Then, when slips, sins, and scandals occur, it is as if the world has changed drastically or a deception has been perpetrated. In fact, the clay feet were probably there all along. Yet, not knowing quite how to live with them or unable to accept their incongruity with the ideal, many of us, lay and ordained, have conspired to conceal them.

So, George, uncertain about his own clay feet which have become increasingly obvious to him with the passage of time and feeling inadequate in the face of an inflated ideal, strives to live out his calling, not quite certain where to turn. No wonder he is discouraged. He faces not only the challenge of declining parish resources but also the personal challenge of teasing fact from fiction and assumptions from reality. At the same time, he must balance his personal hopes and expectations with those of others.

While the traditional ideal may be associated with male clergy, female clergy live with their own set of assumptions and expectations. If a priest is a woman, the challenges she faces in following her vocation may be somewhat different from her male counterparts. Yet, they may be equally daunting. Women have their own share of stereotypes—not the least of which are related to whether they should be ordained at all, what their proper function in society should be, what they must be neglecting in order to do what they are doing, or whether they can, or should, manage an institution of any size.

Lest she be forgotten, George has a wife. He and Myra were married in the summer before his final year in seminary. Myra's goals for herself then were to raise a family and work alongside George in a parish. She did both happily for some time. Then, supported by the women's movement in the sixties, she began to think more about how she might develop her own particular skills. Since she enjoyed all things related to books, she completed a degree in library science and became a school librarian. She continues, however, to see herself as part of a team with George. Even so, Myra often feels as if she were straddling at least two worlds. She is troubled by the assumptions parishioners and others make about her. At times when she is particularly busy, she doesn't like it that parishioners expect something from her simply because she is George's wife. On top of this, she feels the weight of George's increasing frustration. He works longer and longer hours. And, when people criticize him (or her) or pass on their expectations of him through her, she finds herself feeling angry and resentful.

The clergy*man* and his spouse are part of a long tradition. The clergy*woman* and her spouse are, in the Episcopal Church at least, a new occurrence. While images and expectations are not the sum of what the ordained ministry is about, they have a power of their own, for better or worse. How clergy, their families, congregations, and judicatories respond to the expectations set before them is likely to have an impact on their individual and collective health.

The "Uniqueness" of Ordained Ministry

Lay people, and even clergy and their spouses, often hold the belief that in some mysterious way ordination transforms clergy and members of their family into persons who are different from others. Are clergy and their families different? Yes, and no. Undeniably, there are ways in which the ordained ministry is different from other professions. While all Christians may be expected to live according to Christ's teachings, clergy are the people who, in their everyday personal and professional lives, have traditionally symbolized this for others. Perhaps, by association, they acquire an aura of holiness which extends to their families, and sets them apart. Urban Holmes III, in *The Priest in Community* describes the priest as a symbol of the divine link between Creation which formed us and the world in which we live. That "symbol" is, however, a very ordinary fallible human being.[3] Priests are not meant to be infallible or "holier-than-thou," but, Holmes contends, they *are* expected to "embrace a unique vocation of compassion and clarity of mind that requires a disciplined moral life." Clergy are given a particular power which they are required to accept and understand thoroughly lest that power be abused. Then, too, if clergy and laity operate from a narrow understanding of what being a "symbol" means rather than from a fuller understanding of the human and holy dimensions of the vocation, the result might well generate a collision between the vocational life of clergy and their private life (home and family). This impact can affect their capacity to shift readily between the requirements of one aspect of their life and another. Not much imagination is required to grasp the potentially damaging effect such an impact might have. Clergy and their families do have challenges with which to contend. This awesome responsibility suggests that the church very much needs clergy who are healthy.

As does everyone else, clergy have their own set of problems and patterns of behavior that interact with occupational pressures which, in ministry, are particularly demanding. Edwin Friedman, the author of *Generation to Generation: Family Process in Church and Synagogue*, has become a familiar figure to many clergy. He contends that although the ministry may have some unique aspects, the basic issues and events in life which create anxiety are the same for clergy and their families as they are for anyone else. The behaviors that people exhibit when faced with stress are common to clergy and laity.[4] As we will explore in the next chapter, clergy and their families do not necessarily operate in their own best interests when they focus too much on how their situation differs from others.

Unquestionably, clergy need to be emotionally healthy and have a clear sense of what they are called to do and be. At the same time, the vocation they have chosen makes demands of them which have consequences for the systems in which they live and work. Denominational judicatory bodies are frequently called upon to respond to the problems experienced by clergy and their families. Bishops can, and do, play a part in promoting the ongoing health and well-being of their clergy and their families.

The Clergy Family Project

The Clergy Family Project was begun in order to help a diocese create an environment which supports and enriches the lives of its clergy and their families. Both married and single clergy participate in this effort, as well as spouses of clergy. The project is a three-stage process which begins with a period of personal storytelling and discernment, moves to the gathering and interpretation of data from other clergy and spouses in the diocese, and ends with the development of resources for clergy and the families of clergy. An extensive questionnaire, the core of the second stage of the process, helps a diocese gather information about the strengths and needs of its clergy and spouses of clergy. The data from the questionnaire form the basis for this book.[5]

The analysis in the following chapters relies primarily on data obtained from twelve dioceses that participated in the project from 1990–1993.[6] The data, which are computer-analyzed, consist of information gathered from 1,478 individuals. Fifty-eight percent of the clergy who responded are parochial clergy; 58 percent of the spouses who responded are spouses of parochial clergy. The remainder of the sample are non-parochial clergy and their spouses, retired clergy and their spouses, and deacons and spouses. The non-parochial clergy in the sample work on diocesan staffs, in chaplaincies, as pastoral counselors, and in other non-parish settings. Beyond the numerical data, written comments from clergy and spouses provide important qualitative insights. Feedback from consultants who worked with the participating dioceses further illuminates the results.

Health in Mind, Body, and Spirit in Families and in Larger Social Systems

The Clergy Family Project operates under the premise that emotional, physical, and spiritual health factors combine to affect all aspects of the life of any individual. In succeeding chapters the relevance of this holistic approach to the health of clergy and clergy spouses will be described and validated. The interdependence between the overall health of clergy and the health of other family members, both from the past and in the present, is a pivotal focus. This interdependence also extends to the contexts in which clergy and their spouses currently live and work. Clergy and their families do not live in isolation. Their lives are inextricably linked to other events and facets of the culture—local, national, and even international.

Judicatories and congregations, even within one denomination, differ substantially in size, wealth, values, traditions, demographics, and a host of other characteristics that are likely to affect the personal lives and ministries of their clergy. The importance of "external" factors upon a church and its clergy families was recognized at the beginning of the project. For that reason, an exploration of the history, geographic location, demography, and social structure of a diocese is incorporated into the first stage of the Clergy Family Project process. While programs for clergy and families that one diocese develops might be translatable for use in another diocese, factors such as number of clergy, geographical spread of churches, funds available in the diocese, degree of trust and conflict in the diocese, the bishop's recent history in dealing with clergy, etc., will influence the success of any programming a diocese undertakes for clergy and their spouses. For programs and policies to be successful, these factors need to be delineated and taken into account. At the same time, the best planned program falls short if the implementers or recipients are unhealthy emotionally, physically, or spiritually. Hence, the interdependence of mind, body, spirit on the overall health of clergy and their families within the context of their daily life and work is a theme woven throughout the following chapters.

Chapter Two explores the components of overall health and draws on their relationship to one another as hypothesized by mental health professionals, social scientists, and theologians. Chapter Three focuses on the presence of serious problems in clergy families and their effect. The organizations and systems in which clergy function and the effect those systems have on the health of clergy families is the subject of Chapter Four. Chapter Five concentrates on clergy competence and its effect on health. Chapter Six discusses the prevailing issues for clergy who are not among the majority—the majority being male, white, married, parochial. Chapter Seven examines the lives of people married to clergy. Finally, Chapter Eight covers the ways in which dioceses might respond to the issues related to the health of clergy and their families.

CHAPTER II

Health and Wholeness in Clergy Families

Health of family is the single most important thing for the clergy's ministry to be effective.

I believe that taking responsibility for my own health/happiness and for family to do likewise is the very foundation of maturity and health.

ALAN AND JIM HAVE BEEN RECTORS of parishes in neighboring communities for about ten years. Jim is the rector of St. Mark's, a congregation of 400. Alan serves St. Anne's, a church of about 1,000 members. St. Anne's is a bustling place. Attendance is good, growing in fact. Stewardship is excellent. The parish is a stable one with many communicants who have been key to its ministry for a long time. Young families find it attractive. The church school is large, and well-run. Parishioners consider Alan a highly successful pastor. He has boundless energy and many describe him as dynamic, charismatic, spiritual. Parishioners feel comfortable having him as their counselor. Alan has a way of making them feel good about themselves. He always seems available when they need him. An articulate spokesman for many causes, Alan also serves on numerous community and national church committees.

Alan's wife, Mary, runs her own decorating business. Their three children are in their late teens to early twenties. While Alan often appears restless in his "busy-ness," many see it as simply the way Alan is—a condition endemic to energetic, outgoing people. They feel blessed having Alan as their priest. He serves the congregation with devotion.

Jim's story is slightly different. St. Mark's is often referred to as St. Mark's-by-the-Interstate. The congregation is burdened with the maintenance of an aging edifice that nibbles away at the endowment. Though it has a long and noble history, St. Mark's does not attract people in the way St. Anne's does. Still, the community knows it as a church which makes a valuable contribution to the city by housing several service groups. Its members are actively involved in many community projects. Parishioners say Jim isn't flashy, but he is a good, solid priest who leads the flock faithfully, if quietly. His personality does not attract a stream of superlative adjectives. He runs the parish well in the opinion of the church members and is there when they need him. People know that Jim has been married and divorced, but that isn't much talked about. His children, now grown, appear on occasion. And life goes on.

Life does not go on in the same way for Alan. One day he called a meeting of the wardens of the church and announced, "I'm leaving. All I can say now is that some things have come up that I can't talk to you about right now. I feel as if I have done all I can here, and more. I simply can't go on." Then Alan went home, told Mary and the children he had to get away for a time, and left. Everyone was dumbfounded and asked, "What went wrong?"

What *did* go wrong? Alan's action opened up myriad questions.

Most people had assumed that Alan was a "healthy" person. They were at a loss to understand what brought on his sudden departure. Had he, who helped everyone else, really been so expert at hiding problems, problems which progressively worsened, until the only recourse was flight? Or, was his departure a response to a sudden and traumatic personal or professional setback? How might anyone have helped him? Were there warning signs to which his family, the church wardens, or the bishop might have been more alert? Perhaps problems were mounting in Alan's family or within the congregation that had never been adequately addressed or even named. Whatever the case, Alan had shared little, if anything, of his despair with anyone.

Despite the fact that Alan fled and Jim stayed, is Jim any more emotionally healthy than Alan? Does he truly feel fulfilled at St. Mark's, or is he stagnating personally and professionally? Would it make a difference to the health or effectiveness of either Alan or Jim if they were in different congregations, communities, or dioceses? Would the circumstances or answers to any of these questions be different if either was a woman—a perspective that will be discussed in later chapters?

Despite how beneficial or necessary Alan thought his sudden flight to be, his behavior does not reflect well on his emotional, social, spiritual, and professional maturity. By his actions, Alan has left his family and congregation with feelings of guilt, anger, apprehension, and bewilderment. Whoever follows Alan will face a monumental task in helping this congregation to heal.

Suppose Alan and others who know him personally and professionally had been more aware of what constitutes good health or Alan had been able to talk about the stress he was feeling. He might still have left, but he might have given more warning, worked through the break with the other people affected, and left with less damage to all concerned.

Aspects of Emotional Health

In Chapter One, we began our discussion of clergy health with the challenges that being held up as a stereotype of exemplary behavior might present. Another way in which clergy and spouses feel clergy are different arises out of an expectation that clergy are on call, twenty-four hours a day, seven days a week. Whether this is true or not is not relevant. What is relevant is how clergy and spouses manage perception and reality.

Psychiatrist Karl Menninger suggests that the healthy person is one whose capacity to cope is not greatly diminished by weakness and vulnerability.[7] The implications are that health is not the absence of problems but the presence of skills of sufficient flexibility and depth to meet the challenges of everyday living effectively. In so doing, strength is gained for coping with whatever the next challenge brings. Menninger was a psychiatrist and a committed Christian. In his work he often made linkages between religion and psychiatry. The marks of a spiritually healthy person, which will be discussed later in this chapter, and an emotionally healthy person are very similar. As attributes, they complement each other.

In line with his brother's thinking, Will Menninger articulated seven criteria of emotional maturity. They are: 1) the ability to deal constructively with reality; 2) the capacity to adapt to change; 3) a relative freedom from symptoms that are produced by tensions and anxieties; 4) the capacity to find more satisfaction in giving than receiving; 5) the capacity to relate to other people in a consistent manner with mutual satisfaction and helpfulness; 6) the capacity to sublimate, to direct one's instinctive hostile energy into creative and constructive outlets; 7) the capacity to love.[8]

Yet another theorist whose concepts have particular relevance for the church and clergy is Murray Bowen. Dr. Bowen was a psychiatrist

known for his development of Family Systems Theory. Bowen Theory conceptualizes the emotional functioning of human beings beginning with their complex interlocking family relationships and including their biological, psychological and sociological networks. Bowen
identified eight concepts which are observable in human behavior.[9] A
concept in systems theory that is particularly pertinent to our understanding of the emotional health of clergy is "differentiation of self."
Edwin Friedman, a disciple of Bowen, developed the theory for its
application to the organizational systems in which clergy live and
work. Friedman concludes that differentiation of self is imperative for
clergy, given the pressures of working with people in a congregational
setting. The higher an individual's level of differentiation the greater:
1) the capacity to define personal goals and values independent of
those pulling on you to behave as they want you to, 2) the capacity to
remain non-anxious in the face of such pull, 3) the capacity to have a
range of responses when pulled at, but 4) always remaining connected
to others, allowing for *their* differentiation.[10]

   In their own way, these four theorists all articulate principles that
reinforce the desirability of autonomy, consistency, adaptability, and
mutuality in relationships. Each parallels the thinking of the other.
None of the descriptions of emotional health imply that anybody is
free from internal and external pressures. What is important is the
skill with which we respond to those pressures. Healthy living requires the ability to manage our day-to-day relationships effectively,
and maintain a balance between our personal needs and the needs of
others which grants each emotional space.

   We know that Alan fled and Jim worked on. Yet, few people know
either one of them very well. Alan tends to overpower others with all
his activity. (That is a "hindsight" discovery by some parishioners.) Jim
is more self-contained. We know that Alan was unable to maintain a
happy balance in his relationships. We are not privy to the negative

effect Jim's behavior might have incurred.

Social, emotional, spiritual health are interconnected. Lloyd Retiger, who has written extensively on clergy health, supports a "wholeness trilogy." He underlines the importance of strengthening "the body, mind, and spirit legs" in avoiding clergy "burnout," and developing supportive relationships with others—intimate, social, and professional—to strengthen all aspects of health.[11]

Spiritual Health

For clergy, the spiritual realm is not simply a component of a wholeness trilogy. It is also basic to their vocation and to who they are. Perhaps, that is where health begins. In *Reborn From Above* the late Henri Nouwen, a Roman Catholic priest and clinical psychologist, reminded us that although Christians may be able to shape their own personalities, it is the "Holy Spirit alone [who] can cause us to transcend our psychological personality to become a natural person— transparent to others because we are transparent to God."[12] Strength comes from recognizing this power in ourselves and knowing that power to be the work of the Holy Spirit. Being transparent conveys with it the sense that others can see God through us. Considered in this way, transparent people do not distort God's image for others. On the other hand, people who are unable to recognize the work of the Spirit for the power it has to transform their "psychological personality" may well consume the spiritual and emotional space God intends others to share.

Nouwen's analysis of spiritual rebirth aptly describes the struggle involved in a movement toward spiritual health. He incorporates in his thinking the idea that spiritual rebirth does not necessarily include "peace of mind, inner calm, emotional harmony, easy relationships with others, and a well-balanced personality."[13] That may come as a relief to some. While those elements may be present in a person who is "reborn," they are not what makes a person spiritual. Neither, do they, in keeping with our discussion on emotional health, imply that spiritual people are free from challenge. To the contrary, many holy people are "restless, anxious, hard to get along with, and quite unpredictable in their behavior." At first glance, this might seem somewhat contrary to Menninger's description of a healthy ego. Yet, it certainly fits with our discussion in Chapter One of the fallibility of clergy. Spiritual rebirth, as with emotional health, is not a fixed state but an ongoing journey into knowing who we are.

People, Nouwen says, who are reborn in the spirit are "single-minded" in being able to do what is pleasing to the Spirit of God. Such people are very independent, unafraid of the opinions of others. At the same time, they are in relationship with, and present to, God and others. They feel comfortable with who they are and are able to invite others to feel equally at home with themselves. This begins to echo Bowen's and Friedman's ideas about self differentiation.

Movement toward health requires acknowledging our vulnerability and the common bond of sinfulness and brokenness we share with everyone else. Failure to do so leaves a person closed and defensive, sealed off from self and others.[14] We all know people who, fearful of how others might respond, hide their pain. We also know people who are so intent on sharing their pain with others that they leave little space for the pain of others. Nouwen suggests that a healthier model for managing pain is found in the image of the "wounded healer."[15] The ultimate wounded healer is, of course, the Messiah who has bound his wounds in anticipation of binding the wounds of others. According to Nouwen, clergy are called to this model. Priests who have attended to their own "wounds" are capable of focusing on others and providing a space which encourages and enables others to bind theirs.

In another exploration of spiritual health, Roberta Bondi turns to the early monastic writers to illumine our understanding of prayer. Into her discussion, she weaves psychological concepts which support what we have been saying. Prayer strengthens spiritual health. It helps people "move toward God and each other in love." Bondi also stresses the significant part that a healthy "self" plays in the development of a spiritual life. Early monastics claimed that there cannot be love of others, much less love of God, where there is no self to do the loving. "All love," Bondi says, "requires self-giving." A mistake which is often made is to believe that "real Christian love is of such a self-sacrificial nature that we ought not to have a self at all."[16]

Bondi suggests that clergy are particularly vulnerable to the latter way of thinking and that congregations reinforce them in that belief. Yet, in keeping with Bondi's thinking, when there is no true self present, there is no true love to give away. As a result, clergy may misinterpret the nature of the love they have or misuse the power they have been given. A misdirected understanding of self-sacrifice limits our capacity to understand and interact with each other, the world, and God realistically. Bondi maintains that denial of self represents our inability to claim our uniqueness in God and becomes a source of our wounds. Bondi cites three impediments to the full expression of self: 1) feeling that self-worth is dependent on approval from others, or being liked by others, 2) blaming others for our lack of control, and 3) perfectionism. She views all three as particularly slippery areas for clergy. Clergy can be so "paralyzed by a need for approval that they become unable to stand over against their congregation, to be moral leaders of their people." Perfectionism, a trait which conveys that true value comes not from God but from what one does, snares people in its trap. Then, when failure occurs, the tendency to blame others for what has happened only reinforces a sense in clergy of being the victim of the people they want to love and serve. Such blaming reflects an inability to claim the self and leads to a need in clergy to gain permission from others to take care of their personal needs.

Menninger, Bowen, Friedman, Nouwen, Bondi all describe in language similar, yet different, the goals of a healthful life, and the dangers of not taking care of oneself. None would claim that the journey is an easy one or one reachable by all for all time. As Bondi says, congregations have a tendency to collude with clergy in abetting self-sacrifice. How, then, do clergy avoid falling into the trap of self-sacrifice? Changing others is next to impossible. The only behaviors we can actually change are our own. In doing so, we may provoke change in the behaviors of others. The task for clergy and spouses is to understand better what is required of them to be, and stay, healthy.

The Physical, Social-Emotional, Spiritual, and Vocational Health of Clergy and Their Spouses

What do clergy and clergy spouses have to say about their own health in the areas we have been discussing? In the questionnaire, they were asked to assess how accurately the following set of statements described their present life by indicating whether the statement was true, usually true, usually false, or false for them.

I felt healthy and energetic.
I (did not) feel lonely and isolated.
I felt spiritually whole and growing in spiritual depth.
I felt joy and satisfaction from my work in the church.

Approximately a half to two-thirds of all clergy (parochial, non-parochial, and retired) and their spouses would appear from their answers to be in good physical health. Yet, parochial clergy and their spouses, as a group, were less inclined than those in other categories of clergy and spouses to describe themselves as feeling "healthy and energetic." Forty-eight percent of the parochial clergy and 50 percent of their spouses said they usually feel healthy and energetic, as compared to 58 and 65 percent, respectively, of the non-parochial clergy and retired (but still fairly active) clergy and their spouses!

A majority of clergy and spouses appear to have fairly good social-emotional health. While a clear majority claimed that they do not feel "lonely and isolated," between 34 and 39 percent of the pastors and non-parochial clergy and their respective spouses admitted that they had experienced feelings of loneliness and isolation in the recent past. Clergy who have retired from full-time ministry and their spouses show the best health in this area. Only between 15 and 19 percent of them said that they sometimes feel lonely and isolated.

The spiritual health of clergy and spouses in this survey is also quite good. At least two-thirds reported feeling "spiritually whole and growing in spiritual depth." This was tempered, somewhat, by the admission of approximately a third of the active parochial and non-parochial clergy and spouses that this statement was only "usually true" for them. Indeed, 20 percent or so claimed the statement to be more false than true for them. Given the particular vocation clergy have chosen, difficulties that are experienced in this area could potentially be of concern not only for the people for whom this is the case, but also for congregations and judicatories. Once again, retired clergy and spouses appear somewhat healthier in this area than do other groups of clergy and spouses.

How do clergy and spouses attend to their spiritual needs? From a list of eight activities or events, they were asked to rank the three which were most important to their spiritual life and growth. For the entire sample, four activities were identified as being of highest importance. They are: the sacraments (78 percent selecting), solitary meditation and study (65 percent), sermon preparation or listening to sermons (49 percent), and Bible study group/class (31 percent).

The activities chosen by less than a fifth of the sample were: therapy (16 percent), prayer group or house church (14 percent), meetings with a spiritual director (13 percent), and prayer with the family (12 percent).

Physical, emotional, and spiritual health traditionally make up the health trilogy of all persons. If, as discussed in Chapter One, there exists for clergy a particularly close link between vocation and home, then vocational health, i.e., satisfaction stemming from work in the church, should also be added to the list of important contributors to the overall health of clergy and, possibly, of their spouses. Satisfaction and fulfillment in church work are important for a number of reasons.

First, clergy and their spouses are inclined to view the ministry as far more than an occupation. The church is not just the work place but a setting which calls forth and tests their whole worth. Second, a church includes many parishioners who have their own preconceptions about what the church should do and how the rector or vicar and their spouse and children should behave. Clergy observers and researchers have postulated that the private lives of pastors, their spouses, and their children are intertwined with the pastor's work place—the congregation—to a higher degree than is typical for other occupations. Church members often expect clergy and their families to be models of moral behavior. They watch closely to see whether their standards are met and how. Pastors and spouses are inclined to accept the expectations and scrutiny of parishioners as valid, although they complain about living a "fishbowl" existence and the stress this causes them and their families.[17] A combination of self-generated and externally imposed expectations makes the degree of happiness and fulfillment that clergy and spouses experience within the church a central contributor to their overall health. This perspective is supported by the previous discussion of spiritual health in this chapter.

Fortunately, based on an indicator of vocational health, i.e., how much "joy and satisfaction" clergy or spouses obtain "from (my) work in the church," most of them appear quite healthy. Fully four-fifths of our sample checked that it is "true," or "usually true," that their work in the church brings them joy and satisfaction. Over half the clergy indicated this position is "usually true" for them. Again, active retired clergy and spouses came out on top. Church work is clearly a greater source of joy and satisfaction to active retired clergy and spouses than it is to full-time employed clergy and their spouses. The full percentage distribution for this and other items by priest and spouse and by church employment categories depicts the better health reported by retired clergy and spouses. Note particularly the comparison with pastors and their spouses.

The Overall Health Index

Is it possible to measure holistically the health of parish clergy and their spouses as we have interpreted it? Are the dimensions of health we have been discussing interrelated? The answer to both questions is *yes*. Statistical analyses show that the four statements do indeed form a cohesive index that furnishes us with a way of measuring overall health. Can this health index, given the fourth item, which relates to work in the church, be equally applicable to clergy who do not work full-time in a parish and their spouses? It *can* be, if "work in the church" is also recognized as including specialized ministries on college campuses, in hospitals and prisons, on judicatory staffs, and in social agencies. Furthermore, many non-parochial clergy are affiliated with a congregation in some capacity. This affiliation often involves assisting with worship and other church activities. Therefore, congregational involvement can also be considered a factor in the overall health of non-parochial clergy and their spouses. That involvement, in combination with their specialized ministry, also makes the amount of

Clergy and Spouse Health in Core Areas

During the last year or so,
this has been true of me:

		Usually True	Somewhat Tr	Somewhat Fa	Usually False
1. I felt healthy and energetic. (Number)*					
(509)	pastors	48%	35%	14%	3%**
(323)	and spouses	50	31	13	6
(130)	non-parochial clergy	60	28	9	3
(77)	and spouses	57	34	8	1
(111)	retired clergy	57	23	11	9
(72)	and spouses	65	30	4	1
2. I felt lonely and isolated.					
	pastors	8%	28%	21%	43%
	and spouses	8	31	14	46
	non-parochial clergy	8	26	18	48
	and spouses	8	30	19	43
	retired clergy	4	15	19	62
	and spouses	3	12	17	68
3. I felt spiritually whole and growing in spiritual depth.					
	pastors	33%	48%	15%	4%
	and spouses	29	39	22	10
	non-parochial clergy	36	45	15	5
	and spouses	25	47	14	14
	retired clergy	45	47	6	2
	and spouses	38	51	8	3
4. I felt joy and satisfaction from my work in the church.					
	pastors	55%	34%	8%	3%
	and spouses	41	36	16	7
	non-parochial clergy	58	31	5	6
	and spouses	27	44	11	18
	retired clergy	74	22	3	1
	and spouses	57	25	10	8

*Number in parentheses is number of persons responding
**Reading across numbers usually equals 100%; however, the process of rounding off percentages (e.g., 25.5%) to the nearest whole number can occasionally produce percentage totals of 99% or 101%.

joy and satisfaction that non-parochial clergy and spouses derive from church work an integral part of their overall health.

Clergy and spouses within each group (parochial, non-parochial, and retired) vary in how "healthy" they are, based on the health index. To develop the index, the response to each statement was given a

Overall Health Scores of Clergy and Spouses Responding "Very Healthy"

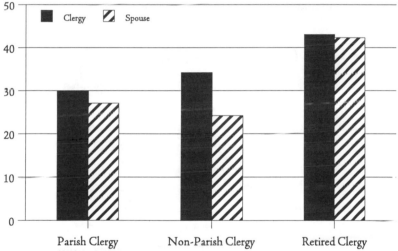

Percent Responding "Very Healthy"

% – % Very Healthy (Scores 4 – 5)

number. True, 1; Usually True, 2; Usually False, 3; False, 4. On the scale of 4 (very healthy) to 16 (very unhealthy), 30 percent of the parochial clergy appear to be very healthy (scores 4–5) while 19 percent are in fair to poor health (scores 10–16). Among spouses of parochial clergy, the percentages at each extreme of the scale are about equal. Twenty-seven percent of the spouses are very healthy and 28 percent are fair to poor in overall health. The full distribution depicts approximately the same range for non-parochial clergy and spouses. Again, retired clergy and spouses appear somewhat more healthy overall. Forty-three percent of them are very healthy.[18]

What makes some clergy or spouses healthier than others? That is a major question for this study and one that this and subsequent chapters will examine in various ways for different groups. The discussion should help clergy, spouses, and dioceses and other judicatories better assess what a healthy life is relative to the profession, what contributes to good health or poor health, and what can be done to safeguard health and counteract dysfunction.

Time: Caring for Self and Health

One answer to the question of why some clergy and spouses are healthier than others is that some simply take better care of themselves. In this survey, clergy and spouses were asked how frequently, in an average week, they participated in a series of activities. Their responses, which range from "rarely" or "never" to five or more times per week, reflect how often clergy and spouses exercise, how much time they spend with a spouse or close friend, how often they socialize with friends for a several hours at a stretch, how often they spend an hour or two alone on hobbies, reading, etc., and how often they devote fifteen minutes or longer to personal prayer and meditation. Among the clergy groups, retired clergy spend the most time in each of these activities. Across the board, spouses are similar to clergy in the amount of time they devote to each activity—except one. On the average, spouses spend substantially less time than clergy do in personal prayer and meditation.[19]

The more frequently clergy and spouses engage in all of the activities mentioned, the better their overall health scores are.[20] One reason that retired clergy and their spouses have better health may be that they spend more time taking care of themselves in these areas. Retired clergy and spouses are usually freer to organize their time as they wish and with whom they wish. Fully employed clergy and their spouses, on the other hand, are likely to have their time limited by job requirements and the needs and demands of their families, congregation, judicatory, and other organizations.

What Do Clergy and Spouses Need to Stay Healthy?

Taking the necessary steps to be healthy is a key factor in achieving good overall health. Lest we imply from our preceding discussion that the solution to being healthy is growing older, age by itself isn't a criterion for good health. Although retired clergy and spouses are in somewhat better overall health than their younger counterparts, age is of little or no importance as a measure of health. This is also true for active (non-retired) clergy and their spouses.

There are a number of steps that clergy and spouses can take to strengthen their overall health. Three activities emerge from the analysis which appear more significant in this regard than others. (Chart I in the Path Chart Appendix indicates statistically how important each type of activity is to overall health.) First, spending time just with one's spouse or, if unmarried, a very close friend is of particular importance for both clergy and spouses, i.e., the more time spent, the healthier one is. Second, the more times during a week that clergy or spouses take at least fifteen minutes for personal prayer and meditation, the better their overall health. This finding is particularly pertinent for spouses of active clergy, although we know from the data that spouses, generally, don't spend time in prayer with great frequency. Third, regular physical exercise is of some importance in clergy health. That is not true for spouses, when considered simultaneously with the amount of time they spend in other activities. Our analysis would suggest that clergy, spouses, parishes, dioceses be alert to the benefit of these activities.

The analysis of the data from the Clergy Family Project supports the importance of emotional, spiritual, and physical health, and the interconnection between the three. To that trio, we have added vocational health. While taking the time to care for oneself is essential to achieving and maintaining good physical, emotional, spiritual, and vocational health, it is not sufficient by itself. Other factors must be considered. Both the amount of time and the degree of personal satisfaction derived from whatever time is spent on an activity may be affected by external factors over which an individual has limited or, in some instances, no control. One such set of external factors will be examined in Chapter Three. Severe problems manifested by other family members are one example of external circumstances over which clergy or their spouses may have some, but rarely sole, control. Although it is possible to reduce the extent to which an individual's emotional health and behavior are negatively influenced by problems exhibited by other family members, the task is not an easy one.

CHAPTER III

Serious Problems in
Clergy Families

My work in this parish seems to be at a standstill. The last year has resulted in the loss of our home and a move back to dependency on the parish for housing. We have one child who seems to have lost himself and one with physical problems which seem to get worse, not better. My wife and I are stretched just about to the limit. Financially, I don't know when we'll be able to climb out of the hole.

SAM'S PARENTS WERE KILLED in a car accident when he was five years old. Fortunately, an aunt, his mother's sister, took him in. Unfortunately, she turned out to be an alcoholic. As he was growing up, he often had to take care of the house, prepare the meals, and care for his aunt when she was drinking heavily. Luckily, Sam was a good student. He went to the state university and then to seminary.

Sam was ordained twenty years ago. He married his wife, Helen, in his last year of seminary. They have three children. For fifteen years they have lived in a small town where Sam has been the rector of Trinity, a church with approximately 150 members. The birth of Sam and Helen's third child almost coincided with their arrival at Trinity. Sarah was born with a chronic physical disability which requires ongoing medical attention. When Sarah reached school age, Helen went back to work. In time, Helen and Sam managed to save up enough money to purchase a home of their own. They bought in a year when property values were rising, but they thought their investment could only increase. Two years later, Sam found himself, literally, flat on his back with a disk problem. Sarah's condition grew worse. Then, their middle child, Eric, was hospitalized for depression. The medical bills became staggering. Finally, they were forced to sell their home. By that time, property values had slumped and they took a loss. Nevertheless, they were relieved to be out from under mortgage payments. Sam and Helen are now back in church housing. Through all of this, the parish has stuck with them and supported them. Sam, however, feels he must work overtime to do what needs to be done. His family seems to need him more than ever. Medical bills are so high that income never seems to match outgo. Sam feels as if he is running in place just to keep up. He is beginning to think that a bigger parish, a higher salary, and a staff of more than a part-time secretary would be the solution to his problems.

Sam had a troubled childhood, but he survived it. He has also faced a string of problems throughout his adult life. Sam can't be blamed for his bad back, his daughter's physical condition, the shift in the housing market, the high cost of medical care, or his son's depression. Yet, trouble appears to be Sam's constant companion. What have we learned that could be helpful to Sam and Helen?

Health and the Family of Origin: Growing Up in a Problem-Ridden Family

In the last chapter, we found that one explanation for why some clergy and spouses are healthier than others lies in the fact that they take care of themselves. In Sam and Helen's case, the question might be posed about the impact that past circumstances have on the present. Growing up in a "dysfunctional" family has become a familiar, though frequently overused, phrase to explain why adults have the problems they do. From a family systems perspective, families develop patterns of relating to each other and the world that are passed to succeeding generations. Those learned behaviors affect relationships either negatively or positively. As positive behaviors will continue to enhance relationships, so problem behaviors will continue to exercise a negative impact until the behavior is understood for what it does and is addressed.

Clergy are no exception.[21] An Episcopal priest being treated for alcoholism in the midst of divorce proceedings states that not all his current problems are attributable to the strains of a demanding ministry. He believes that the fact he "came from a dysfunctional home and had zero self-esteem" contributes in some way to his present personal crises. He suggests that clergy, particularly, may be attracted to the ministry "by unresolved problems in their own childhoods."[22] To what extent is this true? In what way does growing up in a problem-ridden family influence the overall health of clergy and spouses and their capacity to develop family relationships and behaviors which are relatively healthy?

Severe Problems in Clergy Families: Then and Now

One section of the Clergy Family Project questionnaire identifies
thirteen serious problems. Clergy and spouses are first asked to specify
which is *currently* a problem for any member of their immediate family.
Second, they are asked to identify which of them were problems in
their family when they were *growing up*. In neither case are they required to identify the family member. This approach was used inten-
tionally for both theoretical and practical reasons. Theoretically,
although only one family member may manifest a particular problem,
everyone in the family is a participant in it in some way. Alcohol or
drug addiction, for instance, not only ravage the abuser, they also
undermine the behaviors, relationships, and security of an entire
family. Another example is the child whom a family identifies as a
"problem child." That child may, in fact, be "acting out" the pathology
of the family.[23] Practically, however, clergy and spouses often fear that
having a severe problem might jeopardize their church employment
prospects. Even given the confidentiality the present survey process
offers,[24] clergy and spouses find it less threatening simply to check that
a severe problem exists somewhere in the family, without having to
identify the person.

The extent to which clergy and their families have severe problems
may still not be fully known. Some clergy or spouses may be unable to
admit the existence of a problem anywhere in the family for fear that
in some way their disclosure will become public and hurt them socially
and professionally. Second, failure to report a problem is one way of
denying a problem exists. Third, clergy with very severe problems may
not be in the sample at all because they have dropped out or been
forced out of church employment.

The thirteen problems identified in the survey are: severe depression, alcohol/drug addiction, sexual difficulties, children's delinquency,

marital discord, marital infidelity, physical abuse, emotional abuse, sexual abuse, severe physical problems, eating disorders, stress/anxiety attacks, and serious financial debt. Clergy and spouses are encouraged to add any problem not included on the list.

Table 3.1 (next page) shows the percentages for the responses of parish clergy and their spouses only. The same tables were run for non-parochial clergy, retired clergy, and for their spouses. The differences between parochial clergy and their spouses and non-parochial clergy and their spouses are statistically insignificant—a few percentage points at most. On the other hand, retired clergy and their spouses, in keeping with their reputation begun in Chapter Two, do not seem to have as many severe problems as other groups of clergy and spouses, except for "physical problems."

The percentages presented in Table 3.1 show that "frequent feelings of stress, anxiety attacks, or bouts of insomnia" is the problem most often cited for the past and the present. Between a fourth and a third of active clergy and their spouses indicate that someone in their nuclear[25] or present family suffers from severe stress and anxiety. Between 12 and 16 percent of active clergy and spouses say this problem existed for some member of their family when they were growing up. In their discussion of the data, some diocesan committees in the Clergy Family Project have suggested that the higher percentages found in this problem area may reflect that some people find it less threatening to check "anxiety and stress" than to be more specific in naming their problem. Nonetheless, stress, anxiety, and insomnia are conditions which undermine physical, emotional, and spiritual health. Such symptoms may, according to burnout expert Retiger, mark the beginning of "burnout."[26] Thus, severe stress and anxiety must be taken seriously.

Eating disorders, severe depression, sexual difficulties, marital discord, serious financial debt, and alcohol/drug addiction are currently

TABLE 3.1
Severe Problems in Parochial Clergy Families

Now: Please indicate whether you or any member of your immediate family for whom you have personal responsibility has one or more of the following problems:

Growing Up: When you were growing up, did any of these problems exist in your family?

% equals percentage who checked problem as one existing in family when they were growing up or now.

Correlations: Growing Up and Now			Problems Growing Up Clergy/Spouse		Problems Now Clergy/Spouse	
Clergy N=(520)	Spouse (334)					
.30**	.20**	a. Severe depression	16%	18%	17%	15%
.12*	.11	b. Alcohol/drug addiction	22%	23%	10%	11%
.22**	.33**	c. Sexual difficulties	5%	6%	14%	13%
.01	.12	d. Children's delinquency	7%	10%	5%	9%
.16*	.04	e. Marital discord	26%	22%	14%	14%
.14**	.03	f. Marital infidelity	7%	7%	2%	1%
.03	.11	g. Physical abuse	7%	6%	1%	1%
.14**	.19**	h. Emotional abuse	18%	20%	4%	4%
.36**	.21**	i. Sexual abuse	4%	7%	1%	2%
.27**	.01	j. Severe physical problems	4%	5%	6%	5%
.26**	.24**	k. Eating disorders	13%	16%	19%	23%
.27**	.33**	l. Stress/anxiety attacks	12%	16%	29%	30%
.09	.05	m. Bad financial problems	8%	8%	14%	13%
—	—	n. Other	3%	3%	6%	6%

* significant at .01 level
** significant at .001 level

problems for between 8 and 20 percent of the clergy and spouses. Similar percentages show these problems to have been present in the homes in which they grew up. The incidence of marital infidelity; children's delinquency; physical, emotional, or sexual abuse—either now or growing up—were cited by less that 10 percent of our sample.

Clearly, childhood was potentially an unhappy experience for a substantial minority of active clergy and their spouses. Among parochial and non-parochial clergy a good quarter of them remember friction between their parents. Almost that many spouses report growing up in families in which marital discord prevailed. A little more than a fifth of both active clergy and their spouses were reared in families with a member that abused alcohol or drugs. Emotional abuse often accompanied those childhood experiences and is reported by nearly a fifth of the clergy and spouses. Less than a fifth of the clergy and spouses grew up in families in which some family member suffered from severe depression. Eating disorders (severe overweight, bulimia, anorexia) and acute stress or anxiety attacks are problems that 13 to 16 percent of the clergy and spouses in this survey remember from their past.

Some problems either occurred rarely in the families clergy grew up in or, perhaps, were not readily visible to them as children. Few, usually less than 10 percent of the clergy and their spouses, remember (in declining order of occurrence) that acute financial difficulties, children's delinquency, marital infidelity, physical abuse, sexual abuse, and severe physical problems were issues for their families when they were growing up.

Problems that clergy or spouses experienced as children and teenagers may, or may not, recur in today's nuclear family. An analysis of serious problems now and serious problems growing up was done in order to determine whether the same individuals who reported the existence of a particular problem in their families now also report experiencing the same problem when they were growing up. Table 3.1 displays this relationship through correlations.

What the correlations tell us is that the problems which clergy or spouses have now may, or may not, have been problems in their child-hood. For example, it does not follow that all clergy and spouses whose families are presently disrupted by alcoholism or drugs grew up in families in which drugs or alcohol were abused. Conversely, parochial clergy who report that alcoholism was a factor in their family growing up are not necessarily in a family in which alcoholism is a factor now. Although more than a fifth of the parochial clergy and spouses in our study state that some member of their family was an alcoholic when they were growing up, no more than a tenth say that someone in their nuclear family has a severe problem with alcohol or drugs.

In a related item, about a fourth of the clergy and spouses state that it is at least "somewhat true" they feel "the need to relax with a drink with some regularity." Those who admit to using alcohol to relax tend to be married clergy with high family incomes. Statistically, however, there is no correlation between those who "relax with a drink" and those who concede that alcohol is a serious problem for their family. Whether alcohol is a substance they can handle or whether they do not realize that they have a problem with alcohol cannot be deter-mined from this data. Other correlations do show, however, that the families of clergy and spouses who identify themselves as adult chil-dren of alcoholics have a slight tendency to have members who suffer from problems other than substance abuse, namely, severe depression and stress/anxiety attacks.

A few problems that clergy and spouses experienced when they were growing up tend to recur in their nuclear families. Those who grew up in families beset with problems of acute depression, stress/anxiety, and eating disorders are significantly more likely to be in families with the very same problems today. This recurrence appears, however, to be more a matter of *predisposition* than *certainty*. A person who grew up in a family in which these problems existed is only *somewhat* more likely to have the same problems in their family today.

For clergy *only*, there are yet other problems that may be repeated today. Parochial clergy who grew up in the midst of marital discord or infidelity are somewhat more likely to have the same problems in their families now. Similarly, clergy in families with severe physical problems growing up seem to be in families with severe physical problems now. This does not appear to be the case for spouses, however. In fact, the correlations indicate that growing up in a family beset by marital discord or severe physical problems hardly guarantees their repetition in adulthood for this group.

If recurrence of some serious problems is not readily predictable, other problems—particularly sexual difficulties and emotional and sexual abuse—do stand out as "significantly" more likely to be repeated in the next generation. Although these problems are not frequently reported, even a single incident can carry with it extensive and terrible human consequences. Moreover, sexual abuse perpetrated by clergy has become a personal and legal nightmare for clergy, their families, parishioners, and church judicatories.[27] Given that sexual misconduct is an extremely dysfunctional behavior which draws much negative publicity, it may possibly be underreported. In that case, the data may not fully inform us about the possible presence of sexual abuse in pastor-parishioner relationships. Among active clergy, 4 percent (19) of the 520 parish clergy and 6 percent (9) of the 147 non-parochial clergy grew up in families where sexual abuse occurred. Only 1 percent (6) of the parochial clergy and 3 percent (5) of the non-parochial clergy report the presence of sexual abuse in their families today. Two percent of the parochial spouses and 5 percent of the non-parochial spouses admit that they are presently in families where sexual abuse exists. Significant correlations between the answers active clergy gave regarding sexual abuse growing up and sexual abuse now suggest that this is a problem which is repeated in later generations.

And What About Retired Clergy?

As noted earlier in this chapter, a slight majority of retired clergy and their spouses said they grew up, and are currently living, in problem-free families. Aside from "severe physical problems *now*," only 10 percent of the retired clergy and spouses state that any of the other problems listed existed in their families when they were growing up or are present in their families now. The expectation would certainly be that, with aging, physical problems are likely to become factors for people who are retired. As for the other problems listed, either retired clergy and spouses grew up in healthier families than did more recently ordained clergy (a possibility) or they have forgotten some of their early traumas. Another explanation to be considered is that they have lived through, or resolved, many of the problems which now loom large for their younger counterparts.

Measuring Dysfunction

The total number of severe problems present in a family is taken as a rough measure of the degree to which that family is "dysfunctional." Dysfunction is a relative concept, however. The depth and breadth of the severity of any of the problems that families experience varies. Clergy in problem-ridden families—those who report multiple problems in their families—are *assumed* to be in more dysfunctional families than clergy who report fewer serious problems.[28]

As depicted in Graphs 1 A and B, a *majority* of active clergy and their spouses grew up in families in which some member had at least one serious problem. This is also true of their family today. About a

GRAPH 1A
Number of Family Problems Growing Up

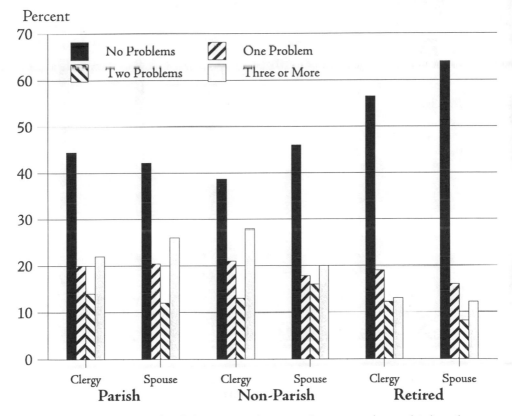

Percent

Legend:
- No Problems
- One Problem
- Two Problems
- Three or More

Parish: Clergy, Spouse
Non-Parish: Clergy, Spouse
Retired: Clergy, Spouse

third (31–35 percent) of the active clergy and spouses (parochial and non-parochial) and slightly over one-half the retired clergy and spouses are in well-functioning clergy families, i.e., those free of severe problems. At the other extreme, families in which there are three or more serious problems (potentially dysfunctional families by our measure) account for a little more than a fifth (21–25 percent) of the active clergy and spouses and about 10 to 13 percent of the retired

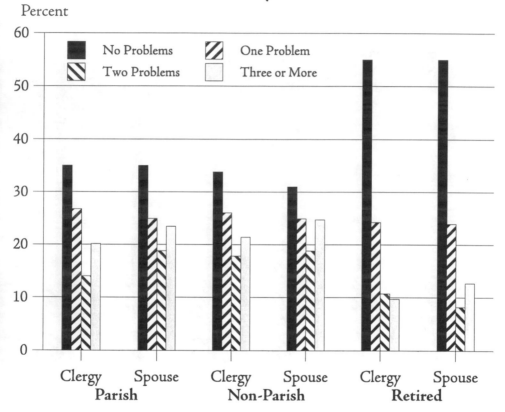

GRAPH 1B
Number of Family Problems Now

Percent

Legend	
■ No Problems	▨ One Problem
▧ Two Problems	□ Three or More

clergy and spouses. Clergy and spouses brought up in relatively healthy families are more likely to form healthy nuclear families than are clergy and spouses raised in problem-ridden families. On the other hand, correlations also show[29] that a substantial proportion of clergy and spouses can form well-functioning families despite the difficulties they encountered by being reared in extremely problem-ridden families.

Dysfunctional Families and Overall Health

The physical, emotional, and spiritual health of clergy and spouses is shaped by the families in which they grew up. Healthy clergy and spouses (as measured by the Health Index scores) are likely to have grown up in families which were relatively problem-free. Yet, what may be of greater significance to the health of clergy and spouses is living in a nuclear family that is problem-free.[30] In fact, if those who were brought up in problem-ridden families have developed relatively problem-free families as adults, they are about as likely as those who have always been in families with no problems to be healthy adults now.[31] A conclusion that can be reached is that, while it may be true that the more problem-ridden the family of origin was the greater the likelihood that adult relationships will be problem-ridden, it is also possible that circumstances will mitigate the transmission of dysfunctional patterns of behavior across generations. Perhaps, as is often true in problem-ridden families, some members do not become enmeshed in negative family patterns of behavior. Or, to borrow from Nouwen's image of the "wounded healer," some have recognized and attended to their "wounds" and, thus, are better able to modify their behavior and relationships with others.

Generally speaking, however, clergy and spouses who are currently in problem-ridden families are less likely to be healthy than those who are in problem-free families. This probability is depicted in Path Chart II (see Path Chart Appendix). Analysis also suggests that severe problems which afflict one or more family members are apt to have negative consequences for the overall physical, emotional, social, and spiritual health of other family members. Thus, it is important to our understanding of healthy clergy and spouses to know *how* problem-ridden, or relatively problem-free, their families are.

In Chapter Two, we suggested that what clergy and spouses do to

Serious Problems and
Clergy Overall Health

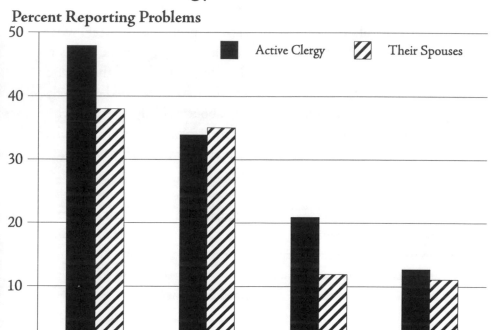

Percent Reporting Problems

Legend: ■ Active Clergy   ▨ Their Spouses

X-axis: No Problems   One Problem   Two Problems   Three or More

Level of Current Family Dysfunction
% = % Very Healthy (Score 4,5)

take care of themselves and the time they set aside for activities which promote physical, social, and spiritual health, help them develop good overall health. We noted in particular the importance of the time clergy and spouses spend together as a couple or in private prayer.

An even better indicator of clergy and spouse health, however, is the problem-free or problem-ridden nature of their households. Yet, this relationship is not without complexity. It is true that the more time a pastor spends just with his or her spouse, the better the pastor's overall health will be even in the face of severe problems. Nonetheless, severe problems exert a very strong force. Thus, time spent is not sufficient, by itself, to transcend entirely the destructive impact that being in a very dysfunctional family exerts on its members. On the other hand, if a pastor does not take time to be with his or her spouse when the family is facing severe problems, then his or her overall health will be even worse. Thus, the task is to find ways to prevent a situation that is already problematic from becoming worse.

Return now to Sam and his wife, Helen, whose story began this chapter. Being able to face their problems together is important to their health. If, despite the physical problems of one child, the emotional problems of another child and their debts and financial crises, Sam and Helen can find enough time for the two of them to be together and talk, they are more likely to be healthy than if they seldom spend time together. The poor health of their children and bank account will still produce stress. Nevertheless, the impact on their own health will be less negative than if they seldom talk, play, or pray together.

In the face of multiple problems, the Sams and Helens of the church may find it difficult to do that which would be most helpful to their own well-being. They may feel controlled by others—parishioners and other family members—who demand a piece of their time. Maybe, too, they have argued so much about their financial problems or how to handle the children's problems that they avoid each other. These feelings and behaviors do little to resolve their problems and will, in the end, undermine their relationship as a couple. Should this continue, will Sam and Helen come to think that the only solution to their problems is divorce?

Divorce

Divorce, although not listed in the survey as a serious problem, is certainly considered one by many judicatory executives. Divorce, when it occurs, creates disruption and pain for the family members split apart by it. Divorce in clergy families also has a negative impact on their congregations and on their relationships with their professional peers and other people in the community. It can also stir up conflict within the diocese or judicatory. This study of Episcopal clergy families began in the mid-eighties out of concern over the divorce rate among clergy. An initial aim of the Clergy Family Project was to help dioceses discover ways to support their clergy and spouses that would lessen the possibility of divorce. The assumption was that the divorce rate was particularly high among clergy and increasing.

The results from the six East Coast dioceses surveyed in 1987 did not, however, uncover a high incidence of divorce. In fact, no more than 8 percent of the parochial clergy checked "divorce" as their current marital status. This percentage reflects a divorce rate which is lower than that for Protestant lay persons.[32] It is possible, however, that the figure we have underrepresents the number of active clergy who are divorced since Episcopal clergy going through a divorce may be forced to give up their parish positions. The survey also does not tell us when a pastor was divorced—before seminary, during seminary, or after ordination. The survey does tell us, however, that many pastors who do divorce later remarry. The divorce statistics found in the present data are not significantly different from those obtained from Episcopal clergy and spouses surveyed in 1987. From the more recent divorce statistics for clergy and spouses, several major points can be made:[33]

1) Although only 6.8 percent of all clergy surveyed in 1991–1992 are currently divorced, four times this percentage, or 24.9 percent of all clergy, have been divorced, at some time.

2) Clergywomen are more likely to be currently divorced than clergymen, especially those clergy who serve parishes. Other percentages suggest that while there is little difference between men and women who are active clergy in whether they have *ever* been divorced, divorced clergywomen are less likely to remarry than divorced clergymen.

3) In looking at the divorce statistics by year of ordination, among those ordained since 1986, a significantly higher percentage of clergywomen either are currently divorced or have been divorced than clergymen. In fact, close to half of the clergywomen ordained since 1986 have been divorced. Most of them have not remarried.

The Impact of Clergy Divorce on Family Dysfunction and Clergy Overall Health

Divorce may be more a problem for the congregation and the judicatory or diocese than it is for the clergy family or for their overall health. Divorced clergy and spouses are just as likely to be "healthy" as those who have not been divorced. There is no relationship among active clergy (parochial and non-parochial) between divorce and health or between divorce and presence of serious family problems.

The Implications of Serious Family Problems

Growing up in a problem-ridden household has a negative impact on the health of clergy and spouses as adults. Particularly destructive is the repetition of family abuse patterns. Substance abuse and abuse of family members (emotionally, physically, sexually) are problems that often repeat themselves in successive generations. What is significant is that clergy and spouses, although they may have grown up in "dysfunctional" families, can enjoy good overall health now if they can create a family life that is relatively free of problems. Many persons, including clergy, manage to survive a childhood marked by patterns of abuse, emotional and physical cruelty, and the seeming absence of adequate parental role models and still grow into emotionally healthy adults.

Problems suffered by a pastor as a child or teenager may heighten his or her ability to recognize and minister sensitively to others with similar problems. On the other hand, those same problems may be ones that clergy as adults cannot tolerate or cope with in others because they react against the "sin" or the "sinner" in themselves. Clearly, as we explored in the first chapter, "wounded" clergy will not be effective "healers" if the problems of the past remain current and disruptive to their personal lives. Nouwen's image of the "wounded healer" who has addressed his or her wounds may then be replaced by the image of a person who has sealed off his or her wounds, perhaps seeking to heal themselves through healing others. Wounds, however, are a part of life. Many great people have had to leap emotional hurdles but have left the world lasting gifts. Being free of illness and problems is not as significant as being able to transcend them.[34]

A happy marriage is important to the overall health and functioning of clergy and spouses. While marital difficulty obviously is a serious problem which can disrupt the family, divorce by itself does not have a negative impact on the overall health of clergy.

When a clergy family has many severe problems, the impact on the overall health of clergymen/women and their spouses will be a negative one. Yet forces outside the nuclear family may also affect the overall health of clergy and their spouses. For all clergy and spouses to some extent, but for parish clergy and their spouses in particular, one force is the congregation. Another is the bishop and others in diocesan leadership. Other clergy, too, may be sources of support or stress. The impact of these extra-family organizations and systems on the health of clergy and spouses is the subject of the next chapter.

CHAPTER IV

Organizations and Systems: Constructive or Destructive?

I work seven days a week, almost never taking an entire day off from work. Recreation consists at most in taking off an hour in the evening to watch one program my wife and I both enjoy. Then I return to my study. Most of all of Saturday I am working toward the next morning's service, running off the service sheet and preparing for the sermon. Some Sunday afternoons I relax, but just as many I work planning . . . future Sundays and other church work. After Sunday morning and feeling criticized by my congregation, I feel driven to try and avoid their future criticisms by 'getting a jump on' my church work. . . . An eight-hour day or a five-day work week seems a joke to me, though it sounds wonderful. At least most of my work is rewarding, just overwhelming.

I think the role of "priest" is mangled by lay expectation and inability of clergy to manage their responses.

It is irresponsible and immoral for the church to expect sixty-hour work weeks from its clergy. This only invites failure in the clergy marriage and family. The church needs to explore alternatives to the values of work and success found within the paradigms of business and academia.

The Nature of Parish Ministry Today

Molly, Doug, and Ken are members of a clergy support group that meets monthly. The three favorite topics of discussion are their parishes, the diocese, and time management. Molly believes that she organizes her time well, as a rule. Sometimes, however, parishioners and the diocese make demands that eat away at her carefully crafted schedule. Occasionally, she gets resentful about that and feels that she doesn't manage her responses as well as she manages her time. Doug thinks of his work as a twenty-four-hour-a-day, seven-days-a-week commitment. He also knows that he must save time for his family. He really wants to do a good job with both, and by juggling his schedule he manages to keep everyone happy, most of the time. Ken gets a bit irritated with Doug. Ken organizes his waking hours into three blocks of time. He works two blocks out of every day in the parish, and takes one and a half days off each week. If some days or weeks require more of his time, he keeps track of the time and takes it later, when his schedule is lighter. He is quite comfortable with this arrangement which has vestry approval. Ken is convinced that few other comparable institutions make the time demands the church does of its employees. He believes the church would do well to look at other models.

Perhaps, as Molly observes, clergy roles *have* become "mangled" by a combination of "lay expectations and the inability of clergy to manage their responses." Many career-focused people choose to spend sixty-plus hours a week at their jobs and as a result have less time for personal relationships. A difference for parochial clergy is that many often feel as if they are, or are expected to be, *always* at work. Such thinking further hinders their ability to differentiate clearly between parish demands and personal and family needs. Are clergy always at work? Perhaps not. Yet, how they manage the church/home relationship has an impact on their spiritual and emotional health and on their families.

In an effort to change their policies regarding clergy job expectation and salaries, churches have, as Ken suggests, been looking more recently at business and academic models. Yet, there was a time when the ordained ministry stood as a witness to vocational dedication. Over a half century ago clergy were less inclined to think of their lives as compartmentalized into "the church" and "the home." Instead, the two were inseparable, with the priestly vocation being the governing element in all areas of life. Some authors have referred to this as an organic-unity model which makes no distinction between the professional and private lives of clergy.[35] This paradigm has been given considerable re-examination for its value to clergy and churches in the last several decades.

In an increasingly fragmented and complex society, the old standards may only heighten the tensions clergy feel as they try to balance the different aspects of their lives. This effort may be further complicated by cultural developments which directly affect clergy and churches, i.e, increased secularization, the challenge to the authority of all traditional institutions, and the greater "professionalization" of occupations. These trends became more discernible in the sixties and continue to shape the culture in which churches exist today.

The same trends also challenge the status of clergy in society today. Although the ordained ministry is still generally respected by society, the esteem and power it once had no longer exist. By the late sixties, the "God is dead" movement bought into question the basic tenets of the faith. Laity began to dispute the authority of clergy and the institutional church to be *the* interpreters of God. This latter trend continues today as church-going lay persons are more inclined to choose which teachings promulgated by their church or denomination they are prepared to accept.[36]

The prestige and authority that clergy may once have enjoyed have also been diminished by professionals in other vocations which require graduate-level education and command salaries considerably higher than those clergy receive. These professionals have also questioned clergy credentials in areas not strictly religious—areas in which clergy have sometimes been engaged by choice or necessity, such as psychological counseling, social work, organizational administration, and finance.

Developments within the institutional church may also contribute to lower clergy prestige. In recent decades, denominational officials and seminary administrators have expressed concern over the quality of people entering the ordained ministry. Of particular concern is the decline in the number of bright, young men seeking ordination. Presumably, this decline is due to better career opportunities in other professions.[37]

Professional Expectations

Alongside the developments in church and society, parish clergy are also being required to assume more roles. Additions to the traditional roles of preacher, teacher, and spiritual counselor include administrator, conflict manager, social worker, community organizer, fund-raiser. Not surprisingly, most clergy find they are unable to excel equally in each area, especially those for which they have no training or expertise. Clergy wrestle, too, with how the ministry of the laity fits in practice with their pastoral leadership and the realities of running a parish. The press of new demands on clergy and ambiguity about the place of religion in society today engenders stress in clergy. The relationship between clergy stress and conflicting role demands was, in fact, a major focus of denominational concern and social science research in the seventies.[38]

In the church of today, clergy must be prepared to juggle a multitude of roles with reasonable skill. Perhaps, "professional manager" would more nearly describe the present model for priests. As historian E. Brooks Holifield suggests, stereotypes of the ideal minister are often drawn from society's image of its cultural heroes and reflect changing social norms and values.[39] In times of change, however, old and new stereotypes often coexist, creating confusion and stress as people adjust their thinking and expectations.

While clergy may take on the professional manager role, the organic-unity model of ministry may also continue to be a paradigm which influences the thinking of many clergy and lay people. Clergy as well as parishioners are often not clear about the overlap of pastoral and personal responsibilities. A philosophy which feeds this dilemma is that ministry stems from divine inspiration, thus making the pastor a person "set aside" by God. While other professionals may also refer to their career as a calling, the calling for clergy is perceived as one from God.[40] Under this awesome condition, clergy and lay people may not want to appear as if they are making a choice between God and their everyday earthly needs.

Clergy of today are expected to be professionally competent, as well as spiritually called to their vocation. All accredited seminaries have pressed to make an advanced degree a requirement for ordination. Most denominations require graduate education as well as spiritual, doctrinal, and personal suitability of its candidates. As in other top-level professional fields, people seeking ordination must pass proficiency exams.[41] Attempts to educate clergy for ministering to today's rapidly changing world often lead to constant curriculum experimentation and revisions and disagreement in and among seminaries and denominations about what clergy need to know and be.[42]

The existence of these cross-pressures suggests that clergy may have more demands placed on them in their profession than other professionals do. Among the stresses most often mentioned are: 1) the lack of clarity in job description and measures of job performance; 2) time management difficulties that thwart the attempts of clergy to establish private time for self and family; 3) the expectation that clergy, and even their family members, be models of behavior for others to emulate. The latter point, the "fishbowl" aspect of ministry, with its implications for the relationship between the congregation and clergy family, is the one often given by clergy and lay spouses as being deleterious to their overall health.[43]

Are Clergy Families "Special"?

Life in a "fishbowl" often makes clergy and their families feel set apart. They feel that they come under greater scrutiny than others in the congregation or community. They are also the recipients of material and social rewards. They receive housing and utilities or a housing allowance which covers mortgage and utilities. Depending on the community in which they live, they may receive "perks" such as memberships in social clubs. Some clergy and spouses look on these as special considerations which are more a curse than a blessing. Often, they put additional pressure on clergy family members to live up to the "favors," or contribute to a sense of being "owned" by the parish. When clergy feel under undue obligation to the people who employ them, they may find it harder to set reasonable boundaries between the job and home, a discussion for the next section of this chapter.

Clergy families may feel as if they are different from other families. Yet, psychologist Edwin Friedman says that "the notion that clergy families are different is a myth,"[44] an idea that is not shared by most of the clergy and spouses in this study. Only 10 percent of the clergy and spouses in our sample—parochial, non-parochial, or retired—disagree with the statement in the questionnaire that says:

Clergy families face some *different* pressures as a *family* than do those families of professionals in secular employ.

The critical discrepancy among clergy and spouses is between those in *strong* agreement with the statement and those who support the statement less strongly or not at all. Fully three-fifths of the clergy and spouses strongly agree that clergy families are different.[45] While Friedman acknowledges that "sociological differences" exist for clergy families, these differences are not the important ones when it comes to understanding the nature of the problems clergy families face or how clergy families function in the face of these problems.[46] The danger inherent in thinking that clergy and spouses are different is that those who believe that clergy families are very different from others tend to shift responsibility for their well-being to others—the diocese, the congregation, other family members—rather than take responsibility for their own well-being.[47]

Do clergy and spouses who think that clergy families are special, i.e., very different from families of secular professionals, have poorer overall health? The answer is a qualified yes. Clergy and spouses who strongly agree that clergy families are *very* different score slightly more poorly on the health index. More to the point, the negative impact on overall health is greater for all lay spouses than for clergy, regardless of gender or status of the ordained spouse—parochial, non-parochial, or retired.[48]

Friedman's observation about the linkage between feeling special and blaming others is upheld. Parish clergy and their spouses who believe clergy families are *very* different are more likely to believe the "Church is responsible for the well-being of clergy families."[49] Having said this, holding the belief that clergy families are "special" is of relatively little importance in overall health when compared to other important factors. One of those factors is found by studying the extent to which pastors and spouses maintain the boundaries between church and personal life.

Maintaining the Boundaries Between Church and Private Life: Negotiating Role Demands

Few pastors would say that juggling the demands of running a parish with the number of hours in the day is an easy one. Many persons, or groups, within the congregation compete for their time. In addition, clergy usually have diocesan and community obligations and expectations to meet, not to mention those of family and friends. Trying to be all things to all parishioners, the "super pastor" would make even a 125-hour week insufficient. It is unlikely that any pastor will be seen as perfect by everyone all the time. Clergy may hope that parishioners and family are reasonable in their demands. More to the point, however, they must learn to set reasonable goals for themselves. When clear about their goals and limits, clergy are better able to communicate their hopes and needs to others, at work and at home. Authors who write about burnout and emotional health concur. Pastors must learn to manage scheduling and role conflicts and maintain some reasonable boundaries between their professional and private lives or risk undermining their health. The task is not easy.

A priest, according to Urban Holmes, is called to be an agent who "illumines" for others the divine and its application to everyday life.[50] At the time of ordination, Episcopal clergy are asked to "pattern" their life (and that of their family, or household, or community) "in accordance with the teachings of Christ" in order to be "a wholesome example" to all people.[51] These are awesome requirements which might lead to the misperception that clergy are society's designated standard-bearers rather than people who lighten the way (i.e., Christ's presence in the world) in such a manner that others, including their families, can follow. The former way of thinking increases the likelihood that clergy and their families will be set apart from others and church and home enmeshed. The latter suggests an action in which clergy are not alone but are joined by others who seek to know God. It also raises the possibility that taking time for self and family is in itself an exercise of faith. Spiritual health requires setting aside time for personal and family needs. The analysis further confirms the necessity of establishing a balance between church and home and affirms the advice given by mental health professionals that clergy and their spouses must maintain clear boundaries between church and private life for their own emotional well-being.

The connection between effective ministry and the capacity to manage multiple roles, schedules, and boundaries is a logical one. Analysis also indicates they are interrelated empirically. The following items from the questionnaire come together to form a scale for both clergy and spouses which describes factors related to their ability to maintain boundaries successfully.[52]

Clergy and Spouse Index of Ability to Maintain Boundaries Successfully [53]

(Scoring: True—4 points, usually true—3, usually false—2, false – 1)

I was able to maintain a separation between my congregational duties and my private life.

I felt I had enough time to do what was expected of me by my congregation.

I felt I had enough time to do what was expected of me by my family.

I felt I had enough time to be alone for reflection, hobbies, reading and recreation.

I felt I did not impose unrealistic expectations on myself.

I felt people in the congregation understood my (and my family's) need for private time away from parishioners and the concerns of the church.

I felt I did not impose unrealistic expectations on members of my immediate family.

The responses to these seven items were tallied for each person answering the questionnaire. Low scores indicate poor ability to set clear boundaries between work in the parish and personal life. Conversely, high scores indicate superior ability to balance role and time demands from all sources and set boundaries successfully.

By this index, clergy and spouses do fairly well setting boundaries on the average. There is considerable range, however, between clergy and spouses in how well they manage their time and role demands. The scores on this scale range twenty-two points, from a score of seven (very poor) to a score of twenty-eight (excellent). The mean score for parochial clergy is nineteen. For spouses of parochial clergy the mean score is twenty. Twenty-five percent of the clergy and 15 percent of the spouses have a score of "fair" at best. At the other end of the scale, 22 percent of the parochial clergy and 29 percent of the spouses of parochial clergy have high scores (24–28) which indicate an adeptness at boundary maintenance.

The greater the ability of clergy and spouses to set boundaries, the better their overall health. Although the scale is most applicable to parochial clergy and their spouses, it is also a reliable indicator of effective boundary setting by non-parochial and retired clergy and their spouses. All clergy and spouses, but especially spouses, who have even slightly above average ability to set boundaries are in better health than those who are less adept in this area. Similarly, those who score extremely high are in even better health than those who are merely "good" at role and time management.

Successful boundary maintenance can mitigate some of the negative effects on overall health stemming from being in a family with serious problems. Severe problems, not surprisingly, make it more difficult for clergy or their spouses to establish clear church/home boundaries and manage their time well.[54] Analysis also suggests that it is particularly important that pastors and spouses whose families are faced with

GRAPH II
Ability to Set Boundaries
and Overall Health

Ability to Set Boundaries

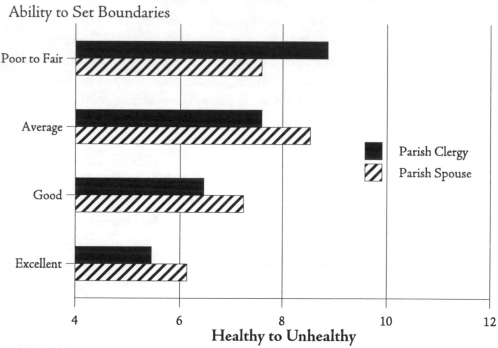

Healthy to Unhealthy

MEAN SCORES ON OVERALL HEALTH INDEX
LOW - VERY HEALTHY; HIGH - UNHEALTHY

serious problems be able to maintain those boundaries and manage their time effectively. The overall health of clergy and spouses in problem-ridden families is apt to be worse than the health of those in

GRAPH III
Family Function and Ability to Set Boundaries on Overall Health
Parochial Clergy

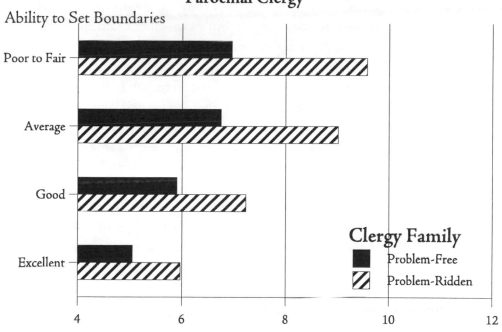

MEAN SCORES ON OVERALL HEALTH INDEX
LOW - VERY HEALTHY; HIGH - UNHEALTHY

relatively problem-free families. If, however, they learn how to set limits well, their overall health will be better. This is illustrated in Graph III above.

"Get a Life"—Or the Importance of a Satisfactory Private and Social Life to the Overall Health of Clergy and Spouses

The survey shows that most clergy and spouses have established happy personal and social lives. Almost all (90 percent) the married clergy and spouses surveyed believe that they are in a marriage which is satisfying to them to some degree. Fully two-thirds said their marriage is very satisfying. And, the more hours a couple devotes to each other weekly, the more fulfilling their marriage is.[55] Caring for home and family is somewhat satisfying for almost all respondents, including single clergy. Nearly three-fifths state that home and family is very much a source of personal satisfaction.

Friendships outside of the family do not provide the same degree of satisfaction that family relationships do. For full-time employed clergy and their spouses, however, the amount of time spent in social activities with friends is important. Perhaps, clergy and spouses find it difficult to develop friendships. Although two-thirds of the active clergy and spouses are *somewhat* pleased with their social lives, less than a third of the parochial and non-parochial clergy and spouses find this area *very* gratifying. Retired clergy and their spouses are significantly more likely to agree that their social lives are fulfilling. That suggests that having free time at your disposal increases the opportunity to develop a social life.

Since a satisfactory social life is more problematic for the majority of clergy and spouses than a satisfactory marriage, is time the element that makes the difference? Not necessarily. The *quality* of the social life may be what makes the difference, because apparently not all the time clergy or spouses spend with friends is enjoyable. Correlations suggest that there are three factors that contribute, positively or negatively, to a satisfactory social life.[56]

1) *Being able to establish boundaries between the church and home.* Clergy and spouses would be wise to establish relationships that are friendship-based, rather than work-focused, with people with whom they can socialize regularly.

2) *The feeling of being different from other families.* The more satisfying pastors and spouses find their social lives to be, the less likely they are to believe clergy families are "special." Those who feel the profession sets them apart and makes them different from others in the church and community may find it hard to establish friendships, however. When this is the case, clergy or spouses may blame their unsatisfactory social life on their position.

3) *Clergy and spouses with fulfilling social lives are less likely to be in dysfunctional families.* The reality for clergy and spouses in such families may be that they have little time and energy to devote to a social life, or they may be ashamed to let others close enough to discover they have problems, or they have found friends to be unsympathetic or unsupportive. Yet, it is important to their overall health that clergy and spouses in families with severe problems find some way to create a fulfilling social life for themselves. The more satisfying clergy and spouses find their social life to be, the better their overall health is. This generalization holds true not only for parish clergy and spouses, but also for non-parochial and retired clergy and spouses.[57]

Overall Health

Earlier discussions of overall health pointed out the relationship between devoting time to various activities, living in problem-free families now, and good health. Path Chart III (see Path Chart Appendix) charts these factors and also shows that two other contributors to good health are the ability to maintain good boundaries between church work and home and having a satisfactory social life.

Additional analysis also supports the other attributes that affect the overall health of clergy and spouses:

1) The amount of time clergy spend with one, or with several, friends affects how satisfactory they think their social life to be. Remember, however, that what is important here is not simply how much time is spent but the quality of the time spent.

2) Hobbies and reading are beneficial to health. This activity, however, has its negative side. Clergy spouses who spend a great deal of time in this way have somewhat poorer overall health. Too much time alone obviously inhibits the development of a social life.

3) Being in a problem-ridden family makes it difficult, but not impossible, for clergy and spouses to maintain boundaries between work and home *and* have a satisfactory social life. Yet, if despite severe family problems, they are able to incorporate these habits into their lives, they will be more healthy.

4) The more time that clergy and spouses (spouses, especially) devote weekly to private prayer and meditation, the better their overall health will be. This is true whether family life is smooth or chaotic.

In each generation, denominations and seminaries are faced with the questions of what constitutes faithful and effective ministry in contemporary society and how best to educate clergy for this ministry. These issues have been of concern to seminaries, denominational executives, and a variety of people responsible for promoting a more realistic approach to training pastors. This approach recognizes the demands of the ordained ministry and acknowledges it as a profession requiring graduate specialties reflective of the tasks performed. With this educational emphasis, clergy may be better able to delineate between the professional role and personal demands. Clergy struggle with their vocational paradigm as societal changes have forced a new understanding about religious institutions and about ministry as an occupation.

Pastors and spouses may face pressures in their vocational setting which are not typical of professionals in secular employment and their families. But the requirements of this occupation do not render clergy and their family members so different from others that they can flourish without good social relationships, or prosper as individuals and pastors without attention to the time it takes to develop a satisfying personal life.

Although parish ministry has somewhat unique attributes, congregations can differ substantially in what they offer, expect, and demand of their pastors and clergy families. Similarly, clergy differ in their competence and aptitude for ministry in particular parishes and communities. How clergy evaluate their own professional competence as pastors under various conditions and the effect that parish setting and perceived competence have on their overall health is the subject of the next chapter.

CHAPTER V

Competent Pastors and Health

WHEN JULIA WAS IN HER MID-FORTIES, she gave up her career as a lawyer and entered seminary. Since her college days, she had yearned to be a parish priest and, when ordination became a possibility for women, her desire became a reality. She took the second job offered her out of seminary. The call to be the vicar of a small parish was just right for her—no corporate rat race, a close community with common goals. Now, five years later, she does not regret her career move, but her initial enthusiasm is considerably subdued by some occupational realities.

Looking back to those first days in the parish, I realize that I was a little naive about what I was getting into. I thought ordination meant preaching and teaching the faith and being the pastor to people in their spiritual journeys and times of need. I thought in leaving corporate law, I would leave administration behind. On the contrary, I spend about as much time in administration in this parish as I did in the law office! What's more, unlike the law office where I had paralegals, accountants, and several secretaries who would carry out my requests immediately and well, here I have only myself and a half-time administrative assistant-bookkeeper.

When I arrived, I discovered that the parish treasurer had been very sloppy in the way he kept the books. It took time to untangle the mess, make sure where all the funds were and that IRS and church reports had been filed properly. The treasurer's family had been in this church for generations. It took great diplomacy on my part not to alienate him and his family, and yet find a way to get a new treasurer.

Though I believe that the ministry of a place like this is a team effort—me and each member of the congregation—I feel that I am the one required to come up with all the ideas, and do most of the work. The youth group is struggling. Families visiting the church for the first time don't always keep coming back. The message I receive from some members of the congregation is that I have failed in my responsibility. I guess I am luckier than a colleague of mine. Her salary is based on the number of new people she brings into the church!

Competence in Parish Ministry

Is Julia an effective pastor for this small congregation? Is the fact that the youth group is struggling due to her lack of skills in that area, or is it that there are not enough teenagers in the community for any church to form a youth group? Would Julia feel any more competent if the congregation were growing, if the staff included a Director of Religious Education to run the youth and other programs, or if there were a committee responsible for welcoming potential new members? The longer Julia stays where she is, will she think of herself as a competent pastor who is doing a good job despite limited resources, or will she begin to consider seriously the possibility of resigning and returning to the practice of law full-time?

The parish clergy in our survey were asked to assess their own effectiveness in fifteen specific areas. To some extent, a majority of clergy see themselves as effective and successful, at least in the tasks they can accomplish without many outside resources. Over four-fifths of the parochial clergy, for example, rate themselves as quite effective in preaching sermons, planning and leading worship, meeting the church budget, crisis ministry, pastoral counseling, visiting sick and shut-ins, teaching adults, designing and administering church programs, and overall parish administration. They do not rate themselves as competent in tasks which depend heavily on the involvement of other persons, such as stimulating parishioners to engage in service to others outside the parish and recruiting new members for the church. Less than half of the parochial clergy see themselves as effective in either of these areas.[58]

Several factors about a congregation influence the way in which pastors assess their capacity to stimulate outreach ministry. Parish clergy are somewhat more likely to evaluate highly their ability to inspire lay members to engage in outreach ministry if they are in churches with good Sunday attendance, strong financial health, growth in membership, a fairly large proportion of college-educated parishioners, or active lay involvement in the church beyond Sunday morning attendance.[59]

Certainly, a shortage of adequate human and financial resources challenges the ability of even the best pastor to minister effectively. Pastors have difficulty indeed stimulating an outreach ministry in congregations that are small, where both church and parishioners are struggling financially, and where the majority of parishioners do little more than attend church on Sunday. A growing church with a solid financial base must help clergy feel as if they are doing something right. Church membership is likely to increase in areas of population growth and in churches with program resources. In fact, when a parish is in good financial shape, the pastor is much more likely to take credit for being an effective financial manager.[60] On the other hand, some clergy may be in larger, financially secure, more active parishes because they are more effective pastors—for that type of parish, at least.

In all tasks but one, the survey data reveal that how competent a pastor feels is not significantly influenced by the number of problems a clergy family has or even how healthy the pastor is overall. This finding fits with Nouwen's thinking on the "wounded healer." Clergy who have problems are *not* necessarily effective or ineffective pastors due to the presence, or non-presence, of serious problems. Perhaps, as Nouwen suggests, they have attended to their problems and are, therefore, better able to be present and helpful to others. A correlation does exist, however, between one area of ministry and the number of serious family problems. The more problem-ridden the family of a pastor is now, the slightly more likely pastors are to rate themselves as very effective in pastoral counseling.[61] This may come as no surprise to those who suggest that clergy come to the profession out of their own need to help others.[62]

Clergy who think that they are very effective in most of the fifteen areas identified in the survey (including, particularly, the ability to stimulate lay outreach ministry and motivate staff and lay volunteers) are more likely to assess their ability to resolve difficult problems or conflicts in their work highly. Not surprisingly, the same pastors are also likely to believe that they are "accomplishing something in their ministry." Most pastors, in fact, indicate that they think they have been fairly successful, most of the time. Nonetheless, three-fifths of the pastors surveyed sometimes feel frustrated by limited resources or the number of people available to do the work that needs to be done in the congregation and community. A third of the pastors admitted that they sometimes, at least, feel bored and constrained by the limits their present position places on their talents and skills.

The Relationship of Competence to Professional Self-Concept

Pastors are able to live with a sense that they are less than competent in a few of the skills required for parish ministry. Yet, if they feel ineffective in a number of areas, are bored, or feel burned-out and unable to meet the basic demands of parish ministry, then the whole image they have of themselves as pastors is likely to suffer. A number of investigators posit that professional self-concept critically affects the ability of practitioners of many professions to manage occupational stress and maintain commitment to their profession.[63] The following items form a cohesive index which appears to measure the "professional self-concept" of the pastors surveyed.

Professional Self-Concept Index[64]
[Each item receives 4 to 1 points (4 – true, 3 – usually true, 2 – usually false, 1 – false as checked by pastors); 4 is low/weak, 16 is high/strong]

I have been successful in overcoming difficulties and obstacles in my ministry.

I have not felt frustrated by the limits of resources or people to do the work needed in this congregation and community.

I have not felt bored and constrained by the limits of this position for using my talents and skills for ministry.

I felt I was really accomplishing things in my ministry.

Over half (57 percent) of the parochial clergy in this study have at least a good professional self-concept (scores of 12 to 16). Only 13 percent have fairly poor self concepts (scores 4–9). This may be good news. Jud, Mills, and Burch, in their study of ex-pastors cited in Chapter Four, speculate that a poor professional self-concept is a major reason why pastors in the United Church of Christ leave the church. According to our data, this potential also exists for Episcopal clergy. The poorer their professional self-concept the more likely parochial clergy are to state that they have seriously considered leaving parish ministry.[65] The fact that only 27 percent say they have seriously entertained this idea recently may be attributable to the average and above average professional self-concept present in most of the clergy in the study.

Pastors with high professional self-concepts also have other things going for them. They are more likely to be in relatively problem-free families, to have satisfying social lives, and to be able to set church/home boundaries than are pastors with lower professional self-concepts. Pastors who fit this description are, no doubt, more likely to receive positive reinforcement from family members and friends than are pastors in disturbed families who feel socially isolated and unable to cope with all the demands that church and home place on their time.

The Effect of the Congregational Setting on Professional Self-Concept

A sense of competence is important to the development of a strong professional self-concept. Thus, the characteristics of a parish that reinforce the development of a sense of competence also contribute to a good professional self-concept. Pastors with high professional self-concepts are significantly more likely than pastors with an average self-concept, at best, to be pastors in parishes that are growing, in good financial health, and with many parishioners who not only attend Sunday services regularly but are also active in church groups and committees.[66] In short, strong pastors are likely to be in strong congregations.

Do clergy in large, wealthy, active congregations have stronger professional self-concepts than pastors of small, struggling congregations because they are more competent, or is it that they appear more capable because they have a staff and a cadre of volunteers to whom they can delegate tasks, particularly those at which they are less competent? When a pastor has adequate help, there is less need to assume roles that others can do better and greater freedom to undertake tasks in which the pastor excels. Larger, wealthier congregations also provide another resource that typically has a very positive effect on professional self-concept of pastors. They usually pay a higher salary than small congregations do.

The Effects of Salary and Financial Satisfaction on Professional Self-Concept

Money has influence. The higher his or her salary, the somewhat higher a pastor's professional self-concept is. Further analysis suggests that the key factor, however, is the relationship between salary and standard of living. The dollar amount, per se, is not as important as its value relative to the local economy. The same dollars have a greater purchasing power in some areas than others. A related factor is how comparable the pastor's salary is to what parishioners and other professionals in the community make. When their salary is on a par with others in the church and community, clergy are better able to match the living standards of their parishioners and professional colleagues. When that happens, pastors are more inclined to believe that they can "live comfortably" on their income. That is the element in income which has a stronger impact on their professional self-concept than the actual dollar amount of their salary.[67] Several national trends may, in time, alter the substance of this finding.

Among the professions requiring a graduate degree, parish ministry is not one that pays a very high salary. Still worse for a number of mainline denominations across the country is the fact that the number of full-time parish positions is declining. Although the majority of seminary graduates in the Episcopal Church find full-time church employment, more and more graduate and are ordained each year for whom there are no full-time positions. This is especially true for women. As an article in a national church publication warns, "the familiar ideal of one priest serving one parish is fast becoming a lost dream." By the next century "yoked" or "clustered" congregations sharing one priest or several part-time "worker priests" are apt to become the norm.[68] For now, at least, almost all of the parochial clergy in our sample have full-time positions.

The family income of half of the married pastors in our survey is augmented by an employed spouse. But whether a pastor's spouse earns an income or not has no direct bearing on the pastor's professional self-concept. Neither is his or her self-concept directly affected by the level of the family's total income, significant as that income may be when both pastor and spouse are employed.[69] Only the salary that pastors earn themselves has a direct bearing on how they assess themselves. Yet, a spouse's income does have an indirect effect on the professional self-concept of clergy. The greater the total family income, the more likely clergy are to say they are able to live comfortably. That perception, as we just discussed, does have a strong impact on self-concept. For now, that is good news. Whether this finding will hold up, as two full-time salaries increasingly become a necessity for all families, remains to be determined.

Support of the Bishop and Other Clergy

The most direct source of information about the kind of job a pastor is doing comes from parishioners. Clergy colleagues and the bishop also provide feedback. As is true for judicatory executives in most denominations, bishops in the Episcopal Church have real power over the careers of the parochial clergy in their jurisdiction. Therefore, how much clergy feel supported and affirmed by their bishop may affect how they view their future prospects and what they think of their ability as pastors.

Clergy are divided on whether clergy in their diocese generally feel free to share their personal problems with their bishop without fear of consequences. No diocese is an exception. Similarly, clergy are divided on how well they know their bishop, or their bishop knows them. Fewer than 10 percent of the clergy in any of the dioceses say they know their bishop or that their bishop knows them very well as persons. Apparently, the support that priests feel they have from the bishop is not dependent upon having a close personal relationship with the bishop. For, while most clergy do not know their bishop well, almost half say that they usually feel well supported by the bishop. Only a fourth feel unsupported by the bishop.

Pastors who believe they have a friendly relationship with, and are supported by, their bishop have a stronger professional self-concept than those who feel distant from their bishop.[70] Which comes first —a strong self-concept or a friendly, supportive bishop? This may be a matter for discussion. Perhaps, pastors who believe that their bishop approves of them have better professional self-concepts because the bishop often tells them what a good job they are doing. Or is it that clergy who have strong professional self-concepts are also effective pastors? Maybe their effectiveness is what gains the approval of the bishop and enables them to initiate communication and enjoy a more friendly, supportive relationship with their bishop.

If support from the bishop is of some importance, so is support from other clergy. Pastors who feel supported by other clergy in either their denomination or other denominations have a strong professional self-concept,[71] perhaps for reasons similar to the pastor/bishop relationship. Other investigators have suggested that priests who have a low professional self-concept also tend to isolate themselves from their clergy colleagues.[72] Their self-concept may be so low that either they are unable to relate readily to others, or are avoided by other clergy because they are not easy people to be with. Which triggers the other—low professional self-concept or isolation from other clergy— is not ascertainable from this or other studies to date. The two elements may tend to converge and reinforce each other.

Professional Self-Concept and Overall Health

Are clergy with strong professional self-concepts also healthier (physically, emotionally, spiritually) than clergy with weak professional self-concepts? Feeling highly competent can be both the cause and the result of good overall health, given that "joy and satisfaction from my work in the church" is one of the four measures of overall health in clergy. Indeed, whether a cause or a result or a combination of the two, the stronger a pastor's professional self-concept, the better his or her overall health, as depicted on the following page.

The Overall Health of Pastors

In the preceding chapters the health of all active clergy, whether they work in a parish or in a church-related organization or social agency, was examined. This chapter has explored only the abilities and experiences of parochial clergy for their effect on overall health. We have also looked at other circumstances which may impact the overall health of clergy who are in parish ministry: the congregations they serve; their relationship with their bishop and other clergy; income; and professional self-concept.

From our analysis of the data, we are able to determine that there are six habits and characteristics that have a critical, and direct, impact

GRAPH IV
Effects of Professional Self-Concept on Overall Health

Professional Self-Concept

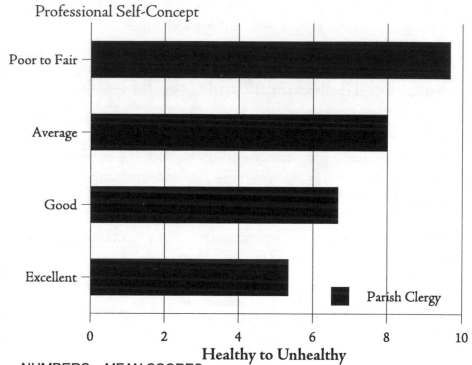

NUMBERS – MEAN SCORES
ON OVERALL HEALTH INDEX
LOW – VERY HEALTHY; HIGH – UNHEALTHY

on the spiritual, physical, emotional health of parochial clergy. They are charted on Path Chart IV (see Path Chart Appendix).

The six items are:

1) A strong professional self-concept. The stronger the self-concept, the healthier pastors are, even considering other important factors that affect their health.

2) The ability to set reasonable boundaries and effect a balance between the demands of church work and personal life.

3) The development of a highly satisfactory social life.

4) Spending time with a spouse or a close friend without anyone else present.

5) The degree to which the family is problem-free.

6) The belief they can live "comfortably" on their income.

It may come as a surprise that a number of factors do not directly influence the overall health of clergy. The amount of time that pastors spend in private prayer does not have a direct impact on their overall health. There is, however, an indirect correlation. Number one on the list above is self-concept. Clergy who have a high professional self-concept also have an active prayer life.

Characteristics of the congregation —size, wealth, degree of lay involvement, location, etc.—are also not on the list because the analysis indicates they, too, do not directly impact the overall health of pastors. There are other factors which appear to have only an indirect impact on the health of pastors. For instance, a sense of competency in specific areas of ministry does not, by itself, have an impact on clergy health. It does, however, increase professional self-concept which, as we know, is one of the direct contributors to good overall health.

Similarly, the level of salary and family income does not by itself contribute to overall health. The key factor is whether the salary is thought sufficient for living comfortably. Of course, a good salary doesn't hurt. And, unless for some reason, such as extraordinary expenses or its inadequacy compared to the salaries of others in the community, the higher a pastor's salary and family income is, the more apt the pastor is to believe that he or she is able to live comfortably. It is this perception which raises professional self-concept which, in turn, contributes to overall health.

Although the support of the bishop and clergy peers may affect how pastors view themselves as parish ministers, their overall health does not suffer without that support if that essential element, a strong professional self-concept, is present. Whether the bishop is someone with whom clergy feel they can share personal problems, or not, also has no direct impact on health. Despite some strong sentiments expressed by clergy in the survey about the pivotal role the bishop plays in the vitality of the diocese, what the bishop does or says has, in fact, minimal impact on the overall health of clergy.

Although a strong professional self-concept heads the list of requirements for overall health, it alone is not sufficient for good health. A satisfying social life is clearly important as well. Being able to "set boundaries" between church and family demands has an indirect as well as a direct impact on overall health because it helps clergy create the satisfying social lives they need.

The good health of a pastor's family always contributes positively to a pastor's health. However, a strong professional self-concept, a very satisfactory social life, the ability to set boundaries between church and home and manage role demands effectively can help a pastor mitigate some of the deleterious effects of living in a problem-ridden family. This is especially true if a pastor regularly sets aside time just to be with his or her spouse.

In this chapter the focus has been on parish clergy, most of whom are married men. In the next chapter, we will be looking in greater depth at clergy who are not in the majority group.

CHAPTER VI

The Many Faces of Clergy: What Can We Learn?

I would hope that the diocese **really understands** *that nuclear families are hardly the norm anymore—and that "family" means different things to different people. I fear "family" often still really is understood as mom, dad, and 2.5 kids. This leaves out single persons, gay persons in committed relationships, single parents, etc. Too often clergy who don't have families that fit the "nuclear norm" are made to feel "second class."*

The diocese and church in general are living with an outmoded myth of clergy as straight, white, male married priests in charge of congregations. The fifties are long gone. It is the nineties, and alternative family structures are a fact of life we must address in some depth rather than putting our heads into the sand. There is a gift of grace in this if the church can be open to accept it.

75

The Changing Image of Active Clergy

Roy, the rector of Christ Church, is white, male, forty-one years of age, and married with three children. Twenty years ago, Roy graduated from an Ivy League university and decided to take two years off to serve in the Peace Corps. That is where he met his future wife whom he married just before entering seminary at the age of twenty-four. A typical clergy family? Not anymore, if we consider others who have been ordained in the last decade and a half.

In all mainline Protestant denominations the most dramatic changes in the last two decades have been: 1) the increasing number of women among the active clergy; and 2) the substantially older age of newly ordained clergy. Although women are still a minority of the clergy in all denominations, there was a rapid increase of women clergy between 1970 and 1988. The proportion of women seminarians in Master of Divinity programs has doubled to the point that now, on the average, almost a third of all M.Div. students are women.[73] The average age of men and women entering seminary has also continued to rise, to the point that it is now about thirty-five.[74] Students who enroll in seminary programs upon the completion of four years of college have become the exception.

When women first became pastors of churches in significant numbers around 1980, they were significantly less likely to be married than were clergymen, either because they had never married or had been divorced.[75] In 1985, the statistics on seminarians showed only 37 percent of the women in seminary were married, compared to 68 percent of the men. This trend appears to have continued into the nineties.[76] The 1985 study also showed that women seminarians were also slightly more likely to be divorced. Sixteen percent of the women and 2 percent of the men in M.Div. programs in 1985 had been divorced.[77] A continuing increase of single clergy as well as the "greying" of the clergy may contribute to a further change in clergy family demographics. Clergy families may have fewer children at home in the future.

The trends may paint one picture, but the image congregations have of the person they want to lead them changes slowly. When a congregation calls a new pastor, they start with a profile of the person they want as their spiritual leader. The experience that is typical of more and more congregations going through the pastoral search process was the subject of an article in the *New York Times*, July 1992. The church that was the subject of the article was seeking someone they thought would "embody tradition and offer a steady guiding hand ... a man in his thirties or forties, married, with young children." They were surprised as they looked at their list of possible candidates to find people wrestling with the same issues they were: divorce, two-career families, emotional illness, and substance abuse. As they searched, they devoted much time and energy into coming to a fuller understanding of the expectations they had for their minister. In the end, the person they called was not a man, but a woman. She does fit some of their expectations. She is married and has children.[78]

The Demographics of Clergy in this Sample

Approximately a fifth of the active clergy in this study are women, four-fifths are men. Table 6.1 depicts some similarities and differences between clergywomen and clergymen in our sample. Although a majority of men and women clergy are currently married, a far greater percentage of men are married than women. Clergymen are also more likely to have children living at home. Still, they do not fit the nuclear family stereotype of "mom, dad, and 2.5 kids." The majority of all clergy surveyed are over forty, not an unexpected statistic given the trends in mainline Protestant denominations. The more dramatic finding is that of the clergy ordained in the last five years, only a minority are forty years of age and younger—this is especially true for clergywomen.

As the statistics in Table 6.1 (See following page.) indicate, of the clergy ordained in the last five years, women are more than twice as likely as men to be over age fifty. Almost all clergy who are newly ordained now are people entering a second career, which may be a new norm for the nineties in mainline denominations—a norm more true for women than men.

The numbers of non-parochial clergy, single clergy, racial/ethnic clergy, and gay/lesbian clergy have probably remained stable over the last several decades. What is new in some areas of the country is that each of these clergy minorities are finding a group voice and protesting unequal treatment by other clergy and judicatory executives. If there are other groups whose rumblings are not heard, their numbers may be too small, their voice may be suppressed by regional attitudes, or there may be too much diversity within the group to give a united voice to feelings of isolation and exclusion.

Non-Parochial Clergy

Non-parochial clergy make up a fifth of the clergy surveyed. Their primary employment is in other church-related jobs or in secular organizations. When employed by the church, they are often chaplains (hospital, prison, nursing home), campus ministers, professional staff members of regional and national church organizations (dioceses, church social service, and educational outreach agencies), faculty members and administrators of church-operated day schools and seminaries. Non-parochial clergy who work for secular organizations are employed in a range of professions. They may, for example, be psychotherapists, administrators of non-profit organizations, or col-

TABLE 6.1.

Demographics of the
Active Episcopal Clergy Sample

			Clergywomen (N = 138)	Clergymen (N = 529)
A.	Active Clergy			
		Parish Clergy	79%	79%
		Non-Parish Clergy	21	21
B.	Age and Year of Ordination			
	Age:	Age 40 and younger	26%	29%
		41 to 50	34	24
		51 to 60	10	21
		over age 60	30	26
	Ordained:	in last 5 years	25%	9%
		6–10 years ago	48	16
		over 10 years ago	27	75
	Of those Ordained in last 5 years:		(25%)	(9%)
		Age 40 and younger	25%	39%
		41 to 50	25	43
		51 to 60	12	11
		over age 60	38	7
C.	Marital Status			
	Single		35%	12%
	Married		65	88
			100%	100%
	Part of Clergy Couple		14% (20)	4% (23)
	Ever Divorced—Total		30 (41)	27 (142)
	Ever Divorced—among clergy ordained within last decade		25 (34)	7 (38)
D.	Children At Home			
	No Children at Home		62%	47%
	Marital status and children at home:			
	Single			
	No children at home		77%	81%
	One or more children at home		23	19
			100%	100%
			(35)	(64)
	Married			
	No children at home		56%	42%
	One or more children at home		44	58
			100%	100%
			(103)	(465)

lege professors. The church work they do—Sunday supply, consultancy, committee member, as examples—is secondary to their primary profession and may be on a fee-for-service or volunteer basis.

Although this study includes only non-parochial clergy who are active in their diocese, it is evident that a great diversity exists in terms of how they exercise their priestly function, and how closely they relate to their diocese. Perhaps, active non-parochial clergy are so diverse and are usually such a small minority of active clergy in a diocese that their particular needs are ignored. At least, that seems to be the opinion echoed in statements by the following non-parochial clergy:

> The church should take seriously non-parochial ministry . . . I would appreciate greater sensitivity in recognizing that 'ministry' or 'priesthood' is not synonymous with *parish* ministry.
>
> Non-parochial clergy need to be valued. Being asked to supply, etc., means giving up free time. This is not very well understood.
>
> Non-parochial clergy should be treated, recognized, and used in the same manner as the parochial clergy. We should all be attached to a parish or mission on a regular basis with regular liturgical and other duties.
>
> I feel that non-parochial priests are misunderstood, under-utilized, seen as second-class citizens, and in general denied a chance to move back into full-time ministry by the establishment.

Non-parochial clergy may derive benefits from their work that parochial clergy do not have in theirs, but there are also frustrations. Non-parochial clergy tend to have somewhat higher incomes than parochial clergy. On the other hand, they do not receive the housing (or housing allowance) and utilities parochial clergy do. Perhaps for this reason, they are no more likely than pastors to say they are able to "live comfortably" on their income. The positions held by non-parochial clergy, particularly in secular organizations, are often very demanding. Thus, demands made on their time by the church may, as suggested in one of the quotes above, be an encroachment on their free time. That clergy are ordained, but not available for parish work on a regular basis, may contribute to a misunderstanding between non-parochial clergy and others in the church.

Particularly irritating to many non-parochial clergy is the lower status they have within a diocese, compared with clergy who are full-time pastors. Unless non-parochial clergy hold executive positions in the church, they may well be seen by many of the parish clergy in the area as second-class clergy, or "outsiders." Among clergy in this study, non-parochial clergy are more likely than pastors to agree that: "Priests in alternate ministries (e.g., chaplains, interims) are not given recognition equal to that given full-time parochial clergy." In fact, they are inclined to agree strongly (40 percent non-parochial clergy to 16 percent parochial clergy) with the statement. Another half of the parochial clergy do support the statement but not strongly. This finding would suggest the possibility that non-parochial clergy are accurate in their assessment of the diocesan climate concerning the status of non-parochial clergy. Fifteen percent of all the clergy surveyed said they had no idea how non-parochial clergy are treated in their diocese.

Despite the allegation made by many non-parochial clergy that they are ignored by other ordained persons in their diocese, there is no significant difference between them and parochial clergy regarding how supported they feel by the bishop and other clergy. Possibly, this is due to the diversity found among non-parochial clergy. Although non-parochial clergy may feel ignored by parochial clergy, many apparently receive support from clergy in the diocese or region. Furthermore, like parochial clergy, some non-parochial clergy have been able to establish better relationships with their bishop than others. In fact, the amount of support non-parochial clergy receive from other clergy and the bishop is comparable to that received by parochial clergy. Furthermore, as discussed in Chapter Two, the two groups are almost equal in their overall health scores.

Single Clergy

Fully a fourth (25 percent) of the active clergy in this study said they do not know whether "single clergy are well-integrated into the fellowship of the diocese." Among those who said they did know, fully three-fifths indicated they believe that single clergy are, to some extent, included in the life of the diocese. Yet, fewer than a fifth held this view strongly, leading to some question about how aware clergy are of the experience of the various groups of clergy in the diocese. The majority of active clergy in our sample are married—three-fifths or more in every diocese. Married clergy often have their social life with other married clergy. Clearly, some single clergy are more involved with other clergy and with the diocese than others. There is no significant difference between the answers given by single clergy and married clergy to the statement that "single clergy are well-integrated" into the diocesan community.

Single clergy are as likely as married clergy to have friends with whom they can talk freely. Their social circles do not, however, involve other clergy families in the diocese to the extent that is true for married clergy. Depending on the area, single clergy form support and social groups with other single clergy in their denomination or other denominations or the community.

Married and single clergy share a general understanding about some of the obstacles confronting single clergy as pastors. Nearly four-fifths (78 percent) of the active clergy "strongly agree" that "Parishioners should not expect single priests to give more time to the congregation than they expect married priests to give." Married clergy are as inclined to endorse this statement strongly as are single clergy. At the same time, while clergy may share the perspective that single pastors should not be expected to do more work in the parish or be overlooked in a pastoral search process, laity on search committees may not. Search committees usually prefer that their potential pastors be married. Furthermore, if there are young children in the clergy household, search committees feel better about hiring a pastor who has another adult to help out. The following quotes represent something of what life is like for single clergy.

> As a single priest, I would be very distressed if support for clergy families would close out single priests. We feel odd enough as it is.

> More respect for single clergy. More real chances for advancement—less patronizing attitude. Diocesan bishops should refuse to allow "single" or "married" be a legitimate category for search committees.

> I see increasing numbers of clergy struggling with the burden of single-parenting. When you are *it* for a parish of wounded, confused children, as well as for a family, the tensions can get incredible.

Indeed, if single clergy are single parents, their social life and private time are probably more limited and circumscribed than for married clergy. A recent phenomenon in the church is the single priest who is a parent to minor children. Divorced clergy are more likely to remain in the ministry than was once the case. In addition, the ordination of women has brought with it an influx of divorced or widowed women with children.[79] Among clergy in this study, 23 percent of the single clergywomen and 19 percent of the single clergymen have at least one minor child. When a single clergywoman is a parent, the financial repercussions are severe, a topic for later discussion.

Gay and Lesbian Clergy

Whatever difficulties that being single creates for clergy in their vocation, their dilemma is made more complex if they are also gay or lesbian.

> Openly gay clergy in committed relationships are *not* accepted; closet gays who play the field are. The hypocrisy bothers me. . . . The Church seems to regard us as anomalous and best ignored. Seems like poor modeling for churches if we want to minister to members in the same situation.
>
> If a single priest has a personal sexual difficulty, especially a homosexual difficulty, he/she will be treated by the bishop differently than a married person with a heterosexual difficulty.

More invisible than single clergy are clergy who are gay and lesbian. Fully a third (33 percent) of the active clergy in this study said they do not know whether "gay and lesbian clergy are accepted by the majority of priests and deacons." Even taking into account that some did not answer the question, this may also indicate that gay and lesbian clergy are not accepted by most clergy and lay leaders in the dioceses in the survey. Only a fifth of the clergy said it is even "somewhat true" that gay and lesbian clergy are accepted in their diocese.

Racial/Ethnic Minorities

Whatever complaints non-parochial, single, and gay/lesbian clergy may voice about their sense of isolation and treatment in their diocese, there is a smaller, and sometimes more silent racial/ethnic group of clergy who could justifiably complain with as much, or more, fervor. Racial/ethnic minority clergy make up less than 5 percent of this sample and most mainline U.S. denominations, as well. This situation has not improved much in the Episcopal Church over the last Wfteen years.[80] Lack of mobility within this denomination for racial/ethnic minority clergy is one reason there are so few in most dioceses. The powerlessness expressed by the following respondent may echo the feelings held by other racial/ethnic minority clergy scattered through the participating dioceses:

> In this diocese if you are a white male priest, you have an unlimited opportunity to move to other churches, even if you totally mess up. If you are a female priest (it helps if you are white), this diocese is the place for you. The bishop seems to really care about the needs of women priests. If you are a priest who is a black male and wants to move to another church, 99.9 percent of the time this means moving to another diocese and starting over again with no money. Now that the white women are claiming to be a minority group—the so-called liberal parishes seem to be hiring them instead of black men, who are most times heads of households.

How Do Clergywomen Fare?

Clergywomen are, indeed, probably doing better in the job market and receiving greater acceptance into the social and professional life of a diocese than are racial/ethnic minorities. Clergywomen are also becoming substantially less of a minority of those ordained. Yet, despite their increased presence within the Episcopal Church, women do not necessarily receive positions and salaries that are equal to those received by the men ordained in the same time period they were. A study of the church positions held by a national sample of Episcopal clergy showed that, in 1985, newly ordained men secured positions which had a substantially higher level of authority and prestige. Furthermore, men were considerably more likely to find full-time entry-level jobs than were women.[81]

Episcopal clergywomen surveyed for the present study receive lower church salaries than clergymen. This may be due, in part, to the fact that men have been in the profession longer. Most of the men in the survey have been ordained for more than ten years, while very few of the women have been ordained that long. For both women and men, the more years they have been ordained, the higher their salary. Yet, among clergy who have been ordained the same length of time, men still command higher salaries than women. For example, a look at just the parochial clergy ordained in the last five years shows that 67 percent of the women make under $20,000 cash salary, as compared to only 54 percent of the men. Of the women and men who have been ordained between six and twelve years, 33 percent of the women make a salary that low, while only 19 percent of the men do. In other words, clergymen continue to get higher salaries and better positions than clergywomen regardless of experience, parochial or non-parochial.

More women than men in non-parochial positions state that their diocese does not value non-parochial clergy to the extent it does parish clergy.[82] Clergywomen in non-parochial ministries are often not only paid less than their male counterparts, but they are also less likely to have secure or full-time positions. Women and men who have low salaries anticipated that, when they were ordained, they would have a better standard of living than they actually do.[83]

Despite these drawbacks, the commitment of clergywomen to their vocation and their feeling of competence is the same as it is for clergymen. Furthermore, the clergywomen surveyed usually hold more liberal, contemporary positions on a number of issues that affect clergy and the church. Clergywomen are significantly more likely than clergymen to:

- Disagree that divorced clergy should leave parish ministry.
- Disagree that clergy should work seven days a week and get their family to accept this.
- Agree that parish ministers who become fathers (especially) as well as those who become new mothers should have a leave of absence from the congregation.
- Say they want social relationships outside of the church.
- Express a desire for personal counseling.

These attitudes may represent a newer model of professional ministry than the traditional "organic-unity" model discussed in Chapter Four. Women are certainly less inclined to accept as their model for ministry one that is drawn in the "likeness of men." In addition, having gone through seminary more recently than most of the clergymen in their dioceses, women may also have acquired a different understanding of the attributes of a good pastor.

Clergywomen, Clergymen, and Overall Health; Similarities and Differences

Are the factors which appear to contribute to good overall health the same for clergymen and clergywomen? Path Chart V (Path Chart Appendix) charts the major contributors to the overall health of ordained women and men. For the purposes of this chapter's discussion, we are looking at the factors that are common to the health of *all* clergy, parochial or non-parochial. Hence, what the chart does not include is the professional self-concept factor which was the subject of discussion in Chapter Five, because it was based on the parish as the work location. Nevertheless, a strong professional self-concept is important to the good overall health of both men and women clergy whether they work in a parish or any other setting. Some of the other previously described contributors to good health among clergy are also not included in the chart simply because their impact on overall health is obscured by the stronger effect of other, more immediate, aspects of the analysis.

What attributes, then, do clergymen and clergywoman share, and in what areas are their needs different? The major contributors to good overall health that are common to active clergy (both women and men, parochial and non-parochial) are:

1) Good boundary-maintenance skills.
2) A satisfactory social life.
3) Being able to live comfortably on their income.

Statistically, a sufficient income appears more important to clergy-women than to clergymen when seen in conjunction with other important influences. For instance, a sense of being inadequately paid, as previously described in this chapter, is a by-product of living in a family with problems where the demand for money for health profes-sionals and special services is great. In addition, as authors Mickey and Ashmore suggest,[84] low clergy salaries often create conflict and stress within the families of clergy or intensify other problems. On a very basic level, clergy, as with other people, need to feel financially secure in order to enjoy maximum overall health. Being able to live comfort-ably is certainly only one of the factors needed for good health of clergy, but it is an important one. This is true whether they are male or female. There are, however, other attributes which affect the health of clergymen and clergywomen in differing ways.

Marital Status

In what way does marital status, or lack of it, play a role? While it doesn't have an impact on the health of single male clergy, it does on the health of clergywomen. Single clergywomen have somewhat poorer overall health than do married clergywomen. One of the major reasons for this seems to be that they are less likely to have sufficient income on which to live comfortably. But, if that were the only reason, then financially well off single clergywomen would have as good health as married clergywomen, which isn't the case. Single clergywomen are often the single clergy most left out of the life of a diocese. Single women are sometimes less welcome in social gatherings that include clergy and their wives than single clergymen are. As single parents, clergywomen are not only apt to have insufficient income, they may also have problems juggling home and church demands. Single clergymen seem to be better able to live on their income. But, even when they have difficulty, they also seem to have external supports and fewer obstacles than clergywomen have. In short, while being single affects the health of clergywomen, it does not have an impact on the health of single clergymen.

Being single does not directly impact the health of clergymen, but living in a problem-ridden family does, considered simultaneously with other health factors. On the other hand, living in a problem-ridden family does not directly affect the health of clergywomen. Clergywomen may be better at balancing work, family, finances, and a social life in the midst of family crises than clergymen.

Relationship with the Bishop

As seen in the last chapter, pastors with strong professional self-concepts are able to maintain good health, regardless of how much support they feel they get from their bishop. If, however, professional self-concept is put aside for the purpose of this discussion of the health of *all* clergy, the relationship with the bishop then begins to have a more direct impact on their health, but in slightly different ways. Clergymen are slightly more likely to be in better overall health, all other things being equal, if they feel supported by the bishop. Feeling supported by the bishop has no effect on the overall health of clergywomen, however. It is more important for clergywomen that they feel free to initiate a call to the bishop. An interpretation which might be drawn from this is that being "supported" by the bishop may be felt by clergywomen to be patronizing. Feeling free to call the bishop denotes a degree of professional collegiality, which is particularly important to the health of clergywomen.

The Place of Prayer

Prayer does not appear on the lists of factors contributing to the health of clergymen or clergywomen simply because it is obscured in the analysis by the stronger effect of other factors. What impact, then, does prayer have? Along with spending time with a spouse or close friend as noted earlier, the more time women and men clergy spend in private prayer, the better their overall health is. In fact, correlations suggest that it is even more essential to health that clergywomen devote time during the week to private prayer than it is for clergymen.[85] In looking at the amount of time spent in private prayer alongside other factors in either group, we find that the important contribution prayer makes to overall health is in strengthening a number of other areas of clergy life which directly affect health. A good prayer life, for example, appears to help clergy surmount family problems, manage time and role conflicts, and maintain boundaries between church and private life, as well as develop satisfactory social and collegial relationships. All are paths to good overall health.

Through examining clergy who are not in the majority, we learn more about the special issues confronting women, single, and non-parochial clergy. Ironically, perhaps, this examination also helps us to understand better what particular factors are most important to the overall health of married male clergy. In developing strategies to improve clergy health, it is important for program designers to understand both the direct and indirect contributors to the overall health of *all* clergy. In doing so, the resources created to strengthen clergy in the basic areas of their life and ministry will be much more germane and productive.

What about the health of lay spouses? Surely, their health is also important to the health of clergy. Married clergywomen may well enjoy better health than single clergywomen because they have both the financial and social-emotional support of a spouse. Spouses of clergy are important in their own right as individuals in church and society. Accordingly, the whole next chapter is devoted to lay spouses.

CHAPTER VII

The Wives and Husbands of Clergy

We are recently retired. As a clergy wife I resented it frequently when the church took so much time when my husband was active in parish ministry. But I said very little. I wouldn't do it that way now! I was in touch with my feelings and needs. It was just that I didn't think I had the right to say anything because his work—"The Lord's work in the Church"—was more important. I wouldn't do it that way now!

I have my own ministry to youth in this church, and I would have it even if the priest-in-charge were not my spouse. But since I am a priest too, there are expectations of me that confuse the issue.

I am on call 24 hours a day, 365 days a year for emergency medicine. There is the possibility of family conflict—especially when my spouse is on call as a priest!

As clergy, my day off is Monday and I work most Saturdays. My husband works Monday through Friday and puts in a fair amount of overtime. There are weeks when we rarely see each other. It's a problem we don't know how to solve.

———————————

I wish that male spouses might be helped before the wife is ordained. Many men seem reluctant to "talk out" feelings of inadequacy felt when the wife opts for ordination.

———————————

My wife's ministry is a team effort. I enable her as best I can by keeping house and doing whatever is hard for her to find time for with her parish responsibilities.

TIMES HAVE CHANGED for spouses of clergy. Among the husbands and wives of clergy in this study, there is a range of views about the appropriate role of the "clergy spouse," and the demands of this role. The clergy "wife" has a long history; the clergy "husband" is a very new phenomenon. What are the parallels between the role of clergy wife of the past and now? Do congregations have different expectations of wives of clergy than husbands of clergy?

Clergy Wives in Centuries Past

Margaret Osiander Cranmer was one of the first clergy wives in the Anglican Communion. In the twelfth century, the Roman Catholic Church enacted legislation which forbade marriage for clergy. It wasn't until the Reformation that clergy—those in the newly formed churches at least—were again allowed to marry. Even then, the English church came to accept the marriage of its clergy slowly and inconsistently. Some of the monarchs on the throne of England in the sixteenth century were more tolerant than others. The Six Articles which Parliament enacted under Henry VIII in 1539 threatened clergy and their wives with death if they did not repudiate their marriages. Edward VI was probably the most moderate, but his reign was short-lived. Mary's reign dealt harshly with married clergy and their wives and offspring. Elizabeth I barely tolerated married clergy and their wives. It was years before the issue was resolved.[86]

Not much is known about Margaret Cranmer. She was the niece of a Lutheran pastor in Nuremberg. She and Thomas Cranmer were married in 1532. Given the general objection to clergy marriages, she was not often seen in public in England. When Margaret traveled with Cranmer, she is said to have ridden in an upholstered chest with air holes. During the years the Six Articles were enforced, she was sent back to Germany to live with her family there. Margaret probably returned to England about 1543. Not until 1549 did she publicly sit at the side of her husband. In a few years, Cranmer would be vilified and executed. Margaret then returned to Germany with their two children, and later remarried. During the years she was married to Cranmer, Margaret's life, like that of many clergy wives in England, was often at risk. In short, the life of the clergy wife in the sixteenth century was not a happy one.[87] One change the marriage of clergy brought to the teachings and attitudes of the church was that clergy began to write in defense of marriage. Marriage had been tainted by the church's negative attitude toward sex. The *Book of Homilies* was published in 1662. Among the homilies, which were meant to be read in churches, was one on "The State of Matrimony" which recognized the nature of marriage and the respect and support spouses should give to each other. The perspective that emerged, however, was a "view of women as obedient and mindless partners in a strongly patriarchal, male-centered family."[88] This model prevailed as the dominant one for all wives in the centuries to come.

Current Trends

The changing role of women in society is perhaps the major factor in the revision of the traditional portrait of the pastor's spouse as a housewife whose world revolves around her husband, family, and church. The women's movement of the sixties and early seventies encouraged increasing numbers of women to seek self-actualization by pursuing their own interests or careers. For many women, however, these pursuits did not supplant the traditional roles of wife and mother. More often than not they have been done in addition to them.

A majority of the wives of clergymen in most mainline denominations work at least part-time, as do most of the young and middle-aged women in the congregations their husbands serve. Initially, the need to augment the family income may have impelled the wives of clergy to go to work. Yet, like other college-educated women, which a majority of clergy wives in mainline denominations are, they may also want to have a career of their own.

A more dramatic change for the church is that the ordination of women has added clergy husbands to the ranks of people married to clergy. A few of these husbands may also be ordained, but usually that is not the case. Some clergy husbands are in social service and teaching professions. More likely, however, they are top-level professionals and business executives. Some clergy husbands have jobs that pay even less than the ministry does. Some are "house husbands," who work only part-time outside of the home, if that.

These social trends are reflected in the clergy spouses in this study. True to tradition, over four-fifths of the clergy spouses are wives, as can be seen in Table 7.1 (See following page.). But husbands of active clergy now make up between 13 and 16 percent of the spouses. Among the spouses of full-time parochial clergy, 61 percent of the husbands of clergywomen and 58 percent of the wives of clergymen are employed outside the home.

Clergy Married to Clergy

Sherry and Dan are co-rectors of a large Midwestern urban parish. They met while in seminary fifteen years ago and were married shortly before each of them was ordained. Their goal was to work together in a parish. For the two years following ordination, however, they were assistants in churches near enough to each other that commuting was not difficult. Next, they found a large parish that was able to hire both of them as assistants. Finally, nine years ago they were called to be the chief pastors of the congregation they now serve.

The congregation and Sherry and Dan have been pleased with this arrangement. Sherry and Dan each bring skills to their job which are complementary. Sherry is a good administrator with a head for finance; Dan is an excellent preacher and counselor. Sherry is a program developer and teacher; Dan is very good with the youth group and parish calling. Together, they cover just about all the areas of competence clergy need for parish ministry. And, the parish gets this for the price of one and three-quarter clergy. Now, however, Sherry and Dan think they have done what they can do where they are, and want to move. They have been interviewed by several churches and have not been called. Other churches say they won't even consider looking at them because that means hiring both. Dan has been approached by several calling committees who are only interested in him.

When women went to seminary in substantial numbers in the seventies, they were apt to be in their twenties and early thirties and unmarried. As a result, female seminarians often married male seminarians, thereby producing the "clergy couple" phenomenon, as well as yet another spouse category. Denominations in the late seventies and

TABLE 7.1
Characteristics of Husbands and Wives of Active Clergy

Spouses of Priests Who Are:	Parochial		Non-Parochial	
Spouses' Gender:	Men	Women	Men	Women
N =	(44)	(290)	(14)	(75)
1. Now Employed by the Church	25%	11%	7%	8%
2. Now Employed in Secular Work (full- or part-time)	61%	58%	71%	63%
3. Total Family Income				
a. Under $30,000	24%	27%	7%	11%
b. $65,000 and over	26%	8%	57%	25%
4. "Usually True" Sufficient Money to Live "Comfortably"	50%	32%	75%	45%
5. "Very Important" for Family Financial Security for Spouse to be Employed	54%	47%	64%	57%
6. How Important is it for Spouse to Have OWN Career?				
a. Very important	61%	41%	57%	52%
b. Somewhat important	9%	32%	22%	19%
7. Spouse's OWN Career Goals Given EQUAL (or greater) Priority than Priest's	70%	25%	75%	38%
8. Degree to which Hours Given Church "Personally Fulfilling"	46%	43%	21%	26%
9. Percentage Saying Hours Given "Fulfilling"				
a. Secularly employed	52%	49%	20%	25%
b. NOT so employed	35%	35%	20%	34%

early eighties struggled to find church positions for these newly ordained women and men either in the same congregation or at least
within commuting distance. Much was written at that time about
clergy couples and the particular issues which they confront when they
must balance church and home life. Two-thirds of the married clergywomen ordained in the late seventies were part of a clergy couple.[89] By
the middle of the eighties, however, most of the women and men
entering mainline seminaries were middle-aged. Marriage between
seminary classmates became less common.

A consequence of the "greying" of seminarians is that married
clergywomen are now more likely to have a husband working in the
secular work force, a person whom they married before entering
seminary. In 1980, 31 percent of all women pastors were part of a
clergy couple.[90] Only 14 percent of the women clergy surveyed for this
study are.

There are so few clergy couples represented in the present study
that any meaningful statistical analysis is difficult. Some comparisons,
however, can be made between the findings of this study and the one
done in 1980. In the earlier study, clergywomen married to clergymen
were more apt to say that their spouses are "never or rarely resentful of
the time and energy" they invest in their work than were clergywomen
married to laymen,[91] 75 percent (ordained husband) and 57 percent
(lay husband). In 1980, this finding was interpreted to mean that a
clergy husband, because he was in the same occupation as his wife,
would be much more understanding of the work demanded of his wife
as a parish minister than a secularly employed husband would be. In
our current data, there appears to be a startling reversal. Now, it is
clergywomen whose husbands are laymen who are more apt to say
their spouses are "never or rarely resentful," 71 percent (lay husband)
and 42 percent (ordained husband).

Due to the small sample of clergy couples in the present study, it is difficult to make a definitive statement about why this shift occurred. Possible explanations may reflect the issues that clergy couples face in the church today. Couples have found it increasingly difficult to find jobs together or within easy commuting distance, perhaps because the job possibilities are fewer or congregations are resistant. Then, too, sharing a job in the same profession challenges their capacity to separate work and home demands in a way that is mutually satisfying. Stress may arise when couples find they have less time for themselves or each other or disagree about whose career goals should be given priority.

What accounts, then, for the apparent shift in attitude of lay men married to clergy, and how might that be of some help to clergy couples? In general, there is much more understanding today about the challenges ordained women face, particularly in being parish ministers. Given this, lay men who are married to clergywomen may have a more realistic picture of what is required of their ordained wives in their work—and what its particular pressures are—than they had fifteen years ago. In many liberal Protestant denominations, the judicatory committees that help decide whether or not individuals should be ordained frequently interview and counsel husbands and wives of people seeking ordination. In addition to making the spouse a part of the process, the interview gives clues as to whether or not these men or women support their spouse's decision to be ordained and whether they have any idea about what they are getting into as a "clergy spouse." In short, a man who marries a clergywoman before she is ordained is likely to be far better informed in the nineties about what is demanded of his wife. Given the husband/wife resentment reversal, a question that this information raises but cannot answer is: Do diocesan committees on ministry take particular care to make sure that the lay husband of a woman seeking ordination understands clergy career demands but assume, perhaps, that the ordained husband of a prospective clergywoman automatically understands the issues they will both face?

Some clergy couples in this study and others have worked out very happy and equitable career arrangements. Recent exploratory research suggests the hypothesis that the husband in a clergy couple may appreciate his wife's ministerial career particularly because he finds "something in her ministry that is lacking" in his own.[92] The ordained wife of a clergy couple may show her clergy spouse new ways of ministering to people and administering parishes which enhance their ministries as well as their marriage.

Money and Work: Secular Employment, Financial Security, and the Desire for a Career Among Spouses of Clergy

Clergy wives, according to consistent findings across denominations, worry far more about family finances and having enough to live on than do their ordained husbands. In part, this may be attributable to the fact that they are the ones who pay the household bills. Or, perhaps, their husbands are so focused on their calling that wives are the only ones left to worry about making ends meet.[93]

A discrepancy does not exist between clergy and spouses surveyed for this study regarding how easy or difficult it is to live comfortably on their income. The spouses in this survey are not all wives, however. Thus, there may be a gender factor which contributes to the lack of difference found here. Indeed, this seems to be the case. Clergy husbands are more inclined to say that it is easy to live comfortably on the family income. Clergy wives still tend to worry.

There is a very good reason why husbands, not wives, of clergy are more inclined to believe that they are comfortably well off financially. They are! In families where the clergy spouse is a husband, there is a greater likelihood that: 1) this is a two-income rather than a one-income family; 2) the husband earns more than his ordained wife. Statistically, married clergywomen are apt to be in families with a higher income than are married clergymen (see Table 7.1).

While these facts would explain why clergy husbands are much more likely than clergy wives to say that it is usually true they are able to live comfortably on their income, there are other reasons why spouses of clergy feel either well off or deprived, financially. Correlations indicate that wives of clergymen are more likely than husbands of clergywomen to feel they cannot live comfortably on their income if there are many family problems.[94] Insufficient income and problems at home may work hand in hand to push wives into the work force, as will be discussed.

Employment reinforces financial security. But husbands of clergy in the survey are more likely than their female counterparts to feel, perhaps with some justification, that it is very important to the family's financial security that they be employed, 72 percent to 54 percent, respectively. Total family income is also a factor in the perception of the husbands and wives of clergy that their own salaries are important to family financial security, but perhaps not in the way one might first expect. The higher the total family income, the more inclined husbands are to state that their own salaries are very important to their family's financial well-being.[95]

Both husbands and wives of clergy believe that the major reason they work is to augment the family income and not because it is important to have their own career per se. Still, more than two-thirds of the wives and husbands in the survey believe it is at least somewhat important to have a career of their own. Husbands of parochial clergy are 20 percent more likely than wives of pastors to say that their career is "very" important to them (61 percent to 41 percent). This difference is not found to the same degree between husbands and wives of non-parochial clergy. As illustrated in Table 7.1, husbands of women in non-parochial ministry are only slightly more likely than wives in the same category to believe that having a career of their own is very important, 57 to 52 percent, respectively.

Among the spouses who are employed outside the home, correlations indicate that the major reason they work is for the financial stability of their family. Interest in having their own work and career is a second reason given, however.[96] A likely scenario for wives who enter the work force is that they do so because their family needs the income. But, when they start working and earning money, the rewards are more than monetary. The boost to their self-esteem in bringing home a paycheck, the interest the work provides, the friends and colleagues they make are other rewards that become increasingly important. This interpretation is suggested by other researchers as well.[97]

While a majority of clergy wives work full- or part-time, approximately two-fifths are not employed outside the home. Among wives who are not secularly employed, a slight majority of them (55 percent) would like to be—at least part-time. The wives who say they want to work, but don't, have more minor children at home, more severe problems within the family, and more unsatisfactory social lives than wives who simply say they are not interested in employment. This would suggest that there are circumstances other than increased income that fuel their interest in working outside the home.

Generally, wives who want to work and have a career of their own get some support from the clergyman to whom they are married. When wives describe their ordained spouse as unhelpful, which a third of the clergy wives surveyed do, they also tend to think that their husbands resent the time they give to their own ministry as lay people. Could it be that these women are married to clergymen who feel that wives should put a husband's ministry ahead of their own career and ministry? In truth, husbands of clergy are considerably more likely (45 percent) than wives of clergy to believe that their own career goals are given consideration equal to those of their ordained spouse. Seventy-five percent of the clergy wives in the survey said that the career goals of their husband take priority over their own. Only 30 percent of the clergy husbands said their wives' careers takes precedence.

Results such as these suggest that the expectations that husbands of clergy have of their marriage, and probably of the congregation, can be quite different from those held by wives of clergy. Although lay husbands no doubt have their own set of stereotypes, the clergy wife is the one who has traditionally been labeled on the basis of her relationship to her husband within the context of a parish.

The Clergy Wife

A typology of clergy wives was developed in the sixties by author William Douglas and expanded by Charles Stewart in the seventies.[98] The major relationship patterns described by them are also voiced by clergy spouse respondents in this study.

The Teamworker is her husband's partner in ministry. Illustrative of this are the words one married couple use to describe their involvement in the congregation:

> Spouse: "We support each other's ministries."
> Priest: "She is fantastic and wholly supportive of *our* ministry. This is the key!"

The Background Nurturer sustains her clergy husband both at home and in the congregation. However, she is more behind the scenes than a visible part of a ministry team. This position is illustrated in the comment:

> My lay ministry has always been to support others in leadership and be a witness to a caring community. I was encouraged in this by my clergy hus-

band, and it was accepted by the parish, after they caught on I wasn't going to run the show.

The *follower* wife is a "purer" illustration of this type:

> I am less involved in church work than before my husband was ordained. My ministry now is focused more on my spouse than on the parish.

The Detached Wife may be a wife who is "detached on principle," feeling that she shouldn't be any more active than anyone else in the congregation. The job clearly is her husband's. Another example of the detached spouse is one who opts to cut off from the congregation because she is rebelling against expectations she believes parishioners have of her. The detached spouse was among the most verbal in this present study. The following illustrates the "detached on principle" type:

> I made it clear to the congregation before moving here that I would not be a "minister's wife" and would not do anything special in the congregation.

On the other hand, the angry comments of those who rebel illustrate their detachment from the congregation their husbands serve this way:

> As his wife, I can have no real function in the church. People often thought I was speaking for him. I dropped out entirely.
>
> I don't have a lay ministry for this congregation. If I did, they would have two slaves for the price of one slave. The folks are cheap and the rector and his family are supposed to be poor and bare-footed.

Wives often become "detached" because involvement in the parish is potentially difficult. Of the parochial clergy surveyed, slightly over half of the wives (52 percent) and husbands (55 percent) say that the fact that their spouse is a pastor is a slight hindrance to their own freedom to be involved in a lay ministry within the congregation. Several explained the "facts of life" as a pastor's wife as follows:

The fact of being a clergy wife does not allow me freedom of activity—through no fault of my spouse. There is no way to be "just one of the members"—so I am learning to keep a lower profile than before my marriage to a clergy person."

The fact that my spouse is a priest contaminates all relationships that I have. People do not relate to us on an unbiased level.

Another spouse describes more fully how limiting it is to her own ministry as a lay person to be the wife of the pastor:

I can't serve on the Vestry. I would be more visibly active in the parish if my husband were not rector. His being rector also impedes my involvement in diocesan activity—for example, as a convention delegate, I have to be careful about speaking my mind!

A fourth category suggested by Stewart is the *working wife*. The career-track wife might fit into this category. Professionally her career may parallel her husband's. How she functions in the parish could fit any of the roles described by Douglas. Of course, how much she does in the parish might be circumscribed by her interests and the demands of her profession.

Are clergy wives employed outside the home better able to maintain boundaries between church and home than those who are not, as Liz Greenbacker and Sherry Taylor, the authors of *Private Lives of Ministers' Wives*, hypothesize?[99] Our study indicates that secularly employed clergy wives are no more skilled at balancing church and home demands and time and role management than their at-home counterparts. Researchers Cameron Lee and Jack Balswick suggest that, while a career may help the minister's wife get out of some obligations (e.g., parishioner expectations of involvement in congregational activities), such "freedom from one role constraint may simply result in captivity to another."[100] Working outside the home does not really excuse wives of clergy, as it does husbands of clergy, from giving major attention to their roles of spouse, parent, housekeeper. In fact, wives of clergy who work are significantly less likely to have much "alone time" than wives who do not. This is not true for husbands of clergy.

"My Pastor Is Also My Wife"—
Some Similarities and Differences Between
Clergy Wives and Clergy Husbands

Tom is a business executive in a middle Atlantic state. As the child of a priest he grew up knowing the church very well. He has always been an active lay man. He did not chose ministry as a career, but when his wife was forty she entered seminary. When she became the pastor of a parish four years after she was ordained, they sold their house and moved into the rectory. As a committed lay man, he is involved in the parish in the issues he cares deeply about. He is also very active in his denomination, locally and nationally. When talking about his parish, he is often heard to say, "My pastor is also my wife."

Generally speaking, wives and husbands of parochial clergy value the time they give to the congregation more than wives and husbands of non-parochial clergy do. They also give more time. Despite the difficulties that spouses of pastors may have in freely pursuing their own ministry as lay people, they are more apt to think of the congregation as a place for their ministry than are spouses of non-parochial clergy.

Work is a factor which affects how fulfilling wives or husbands of pastors find the hours they give to the congregation to be. An assumption might be that the spouse who is secularly employed would find the time given to the congregation a source of some irritation or ambivalence, considering the pressures of a job plus family responsibilities. However, the reverse is the case. Parochial spouses, wives especially, who have jobs are more likely to find the time they volunteer in the congregation personally rewarding than do the spouses who are not employed. Why is this so? Perhaps a career gives a wife an identity which is not so closely linked to the parish. Then, the time that is given becomes a matter of choice rather than obligation. Working wives also need to have their clergy husband support their career goals and the decisions they make about the amount of time they are able to give to the parish. Wives of clergy who think their husbands are considerate about this are more likely to find their work in the congregation fulfilling, and they give more hours.

On the other hand, husbands of clergy who believe their careers are equally, or more, important than their wife's ministry, find the time they give to the congregation not particularly fulfilling, and they give fewer hours. Husbands who are happy about the time they give are more likely to put their wife's career before their own. Maybe that describes Tom.

Husbands of pastors, however, are not expected to give as many hours to the parish as wives of pastors are. A study by Laura Deming and Jack Stubbs found that husbands of clergywomen generally do not feel personally compelled to be active members of the congregation to the extent that wives of clergymen are, nor do parishioners expect them to be. Husbands find it easier to separate parish demands from personal and family ones than do wives.[101] Boundary maintenance between church and private life is not the issue for husbands of clergy that it is for wives of clergy.

Husbands can, however, become emotionally involved in the church their wife serves, sometimes more than they realize. Recent exploratory research suggests that, when a clergywoman changes parishes, her husband may find it as difficult to give up his relationship with people in the congregation as clergy wives do.[102] Social relationships with parishioners can be a very important source of support for clergy and their spouses.

The Importance of Personal and Social Relationships for Good Overall Health Among Wives and Husbands of Clergy

A good social life directly impacts the overall health of clergy spouses, just as it does the health of clergy. Although it is healthy for clergy spouses to maintain some boundaries and separation between the church and their private life, it is not good for spouses to become so detached they are cut off from the congregation given that the congregation can be a source of spiritual and personal support. Clergy wives and clergy husbands often make many of their friends within the congregation.[103] Among spouses in this study, lay friends in the congregation are almost as likely to be turned to for counsel as are friends outside the congregation, 70 to 80 percent, respectively. Outside-the-congregation friends are actually thought to be more helpful, however (44 percent compared to 27 percent). While spouses may feel freer to share personal problems or conflicts in the church with people who are not part of the congregation, having friends within the congregation is somewhat more likely to contribute to a feeling that their social life is satisfactory. Wherever they find their close friends, it is important for spouses of parish clergy to have some close friends with whom they can talk freely if they are to maintain good health.

As a good home and private life are essential to the health of clergy, so they are to their spouses. Almost all spouses say their marriages are more satisfying than dissatisfying, and a majority say their marriages are "very satisfying." Parochial spouses on the whole seem more satisfied with their marriages than non-parochial clergy spouses do (see Table 7.1). There is really no difference between the husbands and wives of parochial clergy regarding the satisfaction their marriage provides. Although their small numerical representation in this sample renders generalizations unreliable, it is worth noting that husbands of non-parochial clergy appear considerably more happy in their marriages than wives of non-parochial clergy, and somewhat more happy than husbands or wives of pastors. Perhaps husbands of non-parochial clergywomen get more of the things that appear to make any clergy marriage better—more hours spent with their spouse, a relatively well-functioning clergy family, a good social life, and freedom from being in the pastor family "fishbowl."

Husbands and wives of pastors have an easy time with boundary maintenance and role and time management if 1) their families are without severe problems, 2) they have sufficient time alone, 3) they enjoy the hours they give to the congregation, and 4) they have close friends they can talk to about issues which concern them. The greater their ability to maintain boundaries between church and home, the better the social life and overall health of spouses is.

The Good Overall Health of Wives and Husbands of Pastors

As we did for clergy men and women, we were able to develop a list of factors that have a direct impact on the overall health of the wives and husbands of clergy. (See Path Chart VI in the Appendix.) This chart is only for spouses of parochial clergy because the sample of spouses (particularly husbands) of non-parochial pastors is small. In addition, spouses of parochial clergy are in a different relationship with a parish than are the spouses of non-parochial clergy. The chart shows that many of the same supports that are important to the good health of clergy women and men are also important for wives and husbands of pastors. But, there are some differences.

How wives and husbands of pastors spend their time—i.e., how many hours they spend alone with their spouse or family, on hobbies, or with friends—is important to their health. For the most part, however, the effect of the amount of time spent is mediated through how valuable they find the time to be, with one exception. Personal prayer has a direct impact on the health of wives of pastors, even when other important influences on health are taken into consideration. How many times a week husbands of pastors pray seems not to be as crucial to their health.

Husbands in problem-ridden families are in worse health than husbands in families that are relatively problem-free, even when considered with other important influences on their health. Wives, on the other hand, are able to overcome the negative effects of being in a dysfunctional family if they are supported by others and feel sufficiently supported financially. Marital dysfunction may be a factor which accounts for this difference since husbands, more than wives, report this as one of their serious family problems. Wives may have more support from their husbands in dealing with any of their severe family problems than clergy husbands do. In addition, husbands of women pastors may feel more unable to cope with family problems on top of their own demanding jobs, a circumstance not as typical among the wives of pastors.

The ability of wives and husbands to set clear boundaries between church and home is essential to their health, regardless of their strengths or weakness. Intimate friends and a generally satisfactory social life are also quite crucial to their health. Even with all of the important influences accounted for, when the wives or husbands of pastors feel as if they are able to live comfortably on their family income, that is one more direct and positive influence on their overall health.

Despite the trend toward greater equity for women in society, the role of the wife of a pastor is still more circumscribed than the role of the husband of a pastor is. Furthermore, "husband" is a far more nontraditional clergy spouse status than "wife." There are fewer well-established expectations of what a clergy husband should do or not do in the congregation than there are for clergy wives. This role ambiguity for men married to clergywomen gives them more freedom to define their way of relating to the congregation than women married to pastors typically have.

For such reasons, learning how to set boundaries between congregation and home is more important to the overall health of wives of pastors than it is for husbands of pastors. Having a career has both positive and negative indirect effects on the overall health of wives. A negative impact is that a job outside the home leaves wives of clergy with less time for family and congregation. A job can also make it more difficult for a wife to carve out "alone time" which is especially important to the balancing of priorities and time for church and family effectively. From a positive perspective, having a job adds legitimacy to whatever limits they, not their husbands or parishioners, need to place on time given to the congregation. Furthermore, when wives bring in a paycheck, the family income is raised. Improved family fortunes provide a feeling of financial security in wives and husbands which has a direct positive impact on their overall health. Given the somewhat poor clergy job market and modest church salaries, dual employment of spouse and cleric of either gender may be more beneficial than detrimental to their marriages and ministries.

The next chapter will present ways in which dioceses and other judicatories might intervene to improve clergy and spouse health, as well as provide additional incentives and assistance to strengthen those areas which bolster their overall health.

CHAPTER VIII

A Course of Action

J UDICATORIES AND DENOMINATIONS can promote the
 spiritual, emotional, physical, and vocational health of clergy and
spouses through creating health-sustaining resources, providing
constructive support, and instilling the importance of using preventive
measures. Doing this effectively requires that a diocese know the
particular issues and problems its clergy and spouses encounter in the
different areas of their lives and circumstances, and what resources or
programs best fit with the needs and interests expressed. A diocese
must then know how to communicate and deliver resources so that
they are accepted and utilized by clergy, or by their spouses. Effective
programming and resource provision also involves taking into account
realities of geography, proximity of clergy to one another, financial and
personnel assets of the diocese, and other such exigencies.

The Clergy Family Project is one way that a diocese can bring
greater clarity to its understanding of the health of its clergy and
spouses. The preceding chapters have analyzed the data gathered from
twelve dioceses that participated in that project between 1990 and

1992. The geographic representation extends from Atlanta to Hawaii (see endnote six, Chapter One). The data come from dioceses that are large, small, densely populated, spread out, urban, rural, eastern, southern, midwestern, northwestern. One—Hawaii—is made up of a group of islands. Almost all the dioceses face the financial crunch other dioceses and denominations face. Some dioceses have more financial resources than others. All dioceses have programs for their clergy and spouses, some more extensive than others. The questions that might be asked are whether what is in place is doing what it is intended to do, and what additional resources and policies need to be considered given this time in history and the characteristics of the diocese.

The primary purpose of the data is to help a diocese find out more about the concerns its clergy and spouses have so that the resources the diocese provides do indeed promote the health they and we seek. In these chapters, we have analyzed the data from a number of perspectives, each of which have some bearing on the overall health of clergy and spouses of clergy. The Clergy Family Project, on the other hand, encourages dioceses to interpret their own data rather than depend solely on the diagnosis of an outside person. They do this with the help of a consultant who helps them understand the percentages and explore ways to respond to the concerns that emerge. In this way clergy and spouses become active partners in evaluating the implications of the ordained ministry for their public and private lives and in developing the resources that help address their particular needs and promote their well-being.

The task of interpreting the data lies with a committee which is representative of the clergy and spouses in a diocese. They receive approximately one hundred pages of collated statistics. Without the help of a consultant and organization of the data, the task would indeed be a daunting one. The responses are grouped into nine areas:

support from and interaction with other clergy and spouses, support from family and friends, balancing work and personal life demands, satisfaction in ministry, support and interaction with bishop, serious problems, spiritual concerns, financial concerns, and continuing education. For each of the areas the committee is asked to put into narrative form what they understand the numbers to mean. They discuss what might have contributed to the responses given. What, for instance, from their knowledge of the ordained ministry, the diocese, the region, their communities, their own lives might account for the needs and strengths expressed? Out of this discussion, the committee begins to explore ways the diocese can sustain the evident strengths and address the needs.

The data-interpretation process is enhanced by what committee members have come to know about their diocese and each other in the first, or "storytelling," phase of the project. That segment helps build community and personalize the data. The data shed new insight on what committee members have already experienced, and expand their vision. This knowledge plus their analysis of the data helps the committee shape the proposals it makes to the diocese regarding resources they believe will promote the overall health of clergy and spouses.

Helping Clergy Families Deal With Serious Problems

While the focus of the Clergy Family Project has been on how to help healthy clergy and spouses stay healthy, the dioceses working in the project also become aware that some clergy and their families require extraordinary intervention. Severe problems, especially multiple problems, have a negative impact on the overall health of clergy and spouses of clergy, as noted in Chapter Three. Clergy who grow up in troubled families tend to live in troubled families as adults. Some problems, such as sexual difficulties and sexual and emotional abuse, repeat themselves generation to generation. Families which are faced with the expense of treatment for serious problems often find themselves in serious financial difficulty. They also often have difficulty maintaining good boundaries. While we know that there are many very competent clergy, we also know that the ministry, like other caregiving professions, often attracts vulnerable people. At issue is not so much the absence of problems, but whether the problems have been attended to so that they impede neither a person's ministry nor wellbeing. The data also suggest that if clergy and their spouses can, as adults, create families that are relatively problem-free, their general overall health is much improved.

Severe problems can certainly have far-reaching implications for dioceses, for clergy, and for their families. Clearly, bishops and commissions on ministry must, and do, consider carefully the emotional health of all persons seeking ordination and the degree to which serious problems have been addressed or continue to impinge upon their lives. Psychiatric evaluations are part of the process leading toward ordination. Bishops, when interviewing aspirants, often inquire about their problems growing up. Given the way in which problems repeat themselves, either directly or indirectly, and given the sexual misconduct of clergy that has more recently come to light, this is particularly important information when considering a person for the ordained ministry. A dilemma, of course, is that people may be reluctant to share information which they think will stand in the way of their acceptance for ordination. This is indeed a challenge to judicatory bodies.

The diocesan committees involved in the Clergy Family Project have wrestled with what resources, programs, or policies would best serve clergy families beset by severe problems. Dioceses are also anxious to ensure that disturbed clergy do not harm others. A necessary policy about which committees have become acutely aware is related to sexual abuse. Sexual misconduct has swooped like a whirlwind into the life of the church of the nineties. Early on, a number of diocesan committees recognized the need to recommend the development of sexual abuse guidelines in dioceses which did not have them. Sexual misconduct on the part of clergy creates intense pain for the victim, the victim's family, a congregation, a diocese, a bishop, the family of the pastor accused, and for the pastor. While the harm cannot be undone, guidelines can expedite the church's response.

Committees also explore the possible prevention of serious problems. Stress, burnout, too little money or poor money management, poor time management, and conflict are but a few areas potentially hazardous to health. One- and two-day workshops serve to help clergy and spouses identify areas in their lives which need attention and to do some self-care. When anxiety becomes too great, burnout occurs, finances are badly overextended, and time is unmanageable. For such times, committees have looked to the provision of therapeutic help for clergy, their wives and husbands, and their children.

Easy access to therapy or counseling provides a means whereby clergy and/or spouses can begin to address their problems before they become too great. Some project committees have urged the development of a guide to services that are available in the diocese or region. Other committees have been even more ambitious and actually developed mental health care services which are modeled after employee assistance programs that businesses provide. How these programs are funded and managed varies from diocese to diocese. What they provide is easy, affordable access to counseling.

The employee assistance programs (EAPs) dioceses provide include services ranging from workshops and seminars to counseling to crisis intervention and cover a number of issues (substance abuse, marital problems, job stress, legal and financial problems, depression, anxiety, wellness). EAPs may be external, i.e., provided by a group or agency under contract with—in the case of churches—the judicatory. They can be internal, provided by a staff person employed by the judicatory. Thirdly, an EAP may be a combination of the two—service through an external provider with a staff person who is a professional in the mental health field to screen intake and administer the program.[104] Whatever the type utilized, confidentiality is key to its usage and success. Remembering that clergy tend to feel under job threat if their problems are known, this factor is very important when considering the provision of health care services.

Enriching the Lives of Clergy, Spouses of Clergy

How can a diocese help its healthy clergy and clergy families stay healthy? The foregoing chapters have shown that there are a number of factors that contribute to health that are often interrelated. An imbalance in any of these health components will impose stress on any or all of the other components and affect overall health. While it is possible for strength in one area to compensate for weakness in another, that may only be expedient on a temporary basis. Ultimately, a chain of reciprocal relationships develops which affects the balance and health of the entire system. In like manner, resources or programs which are developed to address a specific concern may also have positive repercussion on other aspects of the lives of clergy and spouses.

Clergy Families

In the Clergy Family Project, the term "family" was expanded to include the households— the private lives—of *all* clergy. The developers of the project felt that an effort of this magnitude should not exclude others in the ordained diocesan "family." If it were to be helpful to the church, the project would need to bring people together in a common effort, rather than divide them.

Children of clergy have not been directly involved in the project, except for the handful of adult children of clergy who have served on diocesan committees. Some people have questioned why that is so. In thinking about that possibility, the designers of the questionnaire decided that it was not feasible to create a questionnaire that could cover all age groups, and there was no consensus on the one age group that should be, or would want to be, included. Generally speaking, resources which improve the overall health of one family member have repercussions for the whole family. Some resources the committees have recommended, such as counseling, are available to the children of clergy. But there are also specific possibilities for including children that dioceses have considered when developing a program or policy. Dioceses might, for instance, consider including the names of children in the diocesan clergy directory. When clergy or spouses are prayed for in a diocesan calendar of prayer, their children might also be included. Meetings which include the parents of young children might also provide baby-sitting. Finally, children might be included in Clergy/Spouse Conferences or conferences geared to families.

Professional Self-concept

A number of elements reinforce the professional self-concept of clergy. Certainly the relationship to other clergy and, in the case of the Episcopal Church, the bishop is thought to be important by many. Being able to manage time and conflict, being pastor of a church that has people and money resources, and experiencing a sense of accomplishment all enhance self-concept. These are elements which dioceses take into account when considering the benefit to be gained from the resources a diocese provides.

Some dioceses are particularly concerned about developing a community of professional support for clergy. They have explored the use of small group gatherings of clergy to act as support groups and mentors to each other. Clergy ordained the same year may meet regularly to act as support for each other. Clergy living near each other may meet weekly to do Bible study, prayer, and sermon reflection. These are resources which can be utilized by clergy. While the ideas may not necessarily be new to some, the data from the Clergy Family Project questionnaire reinforce the benefit of such support and give a diocese the information it requires to tailor its programs.

Clergy are not always aware of the resources that exist in their region for continuing education and spiritual direction. This is particularly true for clergy new to an area. Some committees have developed directories which give the local resources. They also encourage clergy to utilize available diocesan resources and consultants.

An area which certainly contributes to vocational health and increases self-concept and sense of accomplishment in ministry is continuing education. Some clergy make ready use of funds and resources for continuing education. So far, none of the participants in the Clergy Family Project has been in an area that is so isolated that there is not some access to continuing education. The Episcopal Church has no requirement for continuing education for clergy. Several diocesan committees have talked about establishing diocesan policies, procedures, and expectations for clergy regarding continuing education. Some committees also recommend that their diocese make continuing education funds available to spouses.

Boundary Maintenance Skills

A factor which contributes to good boundary maintenance is being in a family that is relatively free of problems. It is also obvious that the greater the demands placed on time, the greater difficulty a person has in allocating time in a constructive way. A satisfactory social life, as well as time to be alone for such activities as reading, hobbies, and the pursuit of other interests also influences the healthy maintenance of boundaries. Although marriage and children may impinge on free time, no one would want to recommend celibacy as a path to boundary maintenance. At the same time, managing time is a special challenge for people who are married and have children at home.

A step forward in time management is to learn to schedule time and set realistic goals and expectations. Some people working on the Clergy Family Project have recommended a diocesan policy which gives clergy two days off a week. Time, thus permitted, creates the space needed for personal interests and family. That may be more easily said than done, of course. "How-to" workshops may help. Clergy can also support each other in this through the small professional groups of which they are a part. On the other hand, professional help may be needed to help clergy give themselves permission to take time for themselves and their family and communicate the need for time off to the congregation. It is important to remember that having time alone with their ordained spouse is important to wives and husbands of clergy. A key issue might be whether clergy can let themselves take the time they, or anyone else, gives them. Anxiety may so overtake people faced with the possibility of free time that the vacuum created may only be filled with more work.

There are certainly some boundary maintenance issues related to being the spouse of an ordained person, specifically to being a wife. Some dioceses have long had Clergy Spouse Conferences and/or support groups. Some are more successful than others. What many dioceses have found is that spouses often prefer conferences in which their ordained spouse is also present, not ones for spouses only. One diocese recognized that having a career and managing a family also places the demands on spouses that it does on clergy. Their instructions for anything their diocese might do to be supportive of clergy spouses includes the warning to avoid putting any more demands on their time by developing programs which require their attendance. Since what seems to be important for working wives is having sufficient time for themselves, their husbands, families, and social lives, then any program developed should incorporate those aspects of their lives rather than further frustrate them.

Satisfactory Social Life

A social life is important to the on-going health of clergy and spouses. While a diocese may be able to create possibilities for clergy and spouses to socialize with other clergy and spouses, it cannot necessarily do anything about their other social relationships except to encourage them.

A number of dioceses have created opportunities for clergy and spouses of clergy to gather on a purely social basis. These may be diocesan-wide gatherings or small group gatherings. Such gatherings also provide professional support on an informal basis. Typically, diocesan-sponsored clergy and spouse gatherings are welcomed by all attending. Clergy/spouse day meetings or overnight retreats not only provide interpersonal support for clergy and spouses, but also enhance their support of the diocese, particularly if the bishop attends. Some dioceses have developed a process of welcoming and orienting incoming clergy and their families to the diocese. Some have also designed handbooks which put information about the diocese and the region readily at the fingertips of clergy and spouses, new and old, in the diocese. Handbooks also connect people with each other, the diocese and the community.

Living Comfortably on One's Income

As described in earlier chapters, living comfortably on one's income is as much a matter of individual perception—personal circumstances and expectations amid the life style of the community—as it is of actual amount of income. Being in a clergy family with multiple serious problems erodes what income there is and also contributes to the apprehension that family problems will demand additional money in the future which will not be available. Judicatories cannot promise clergy financial security, nor can churches typically match the salaries of comparably educated professionals in other occupations. Nevertheless, having adequate compensation is a concern of dioceses involved in the Clergy Family Project. While a number of dioceses have salary guidelines for entering clergy, Clergy Family Project committees also recommend that the guidelines be fully developed for clergy beyond the entry level.

Money management helps clergy families budget what money they do have. Clergy wives worry particularly about money, probably because they are the family budget managers. Yet, national and judicatory offices do not always include clergy wives in financial seminars and mailings sent to clergy. To heighten the awareness of that need, many of the committees recommend that diocesan mailings on any issue that reaches into the lives of clergy spouses and families be sent directly to the home rather than through the church office. Committees also recommend financial planning seminars where none exist. Included in the resources that EAPs provide is counseling for those who have overextended their budget.

Spiritual Growth

Clergy are in the "church business." If they are to be able to translate the faith for their congregation and community, they must grow spiritually themselves. Fortunately, the data indicate that a healthy majority of the clergy believe that this is happening for them. And, it is also happening for their spouses.

Some of the committees in the project have observed that it is easy for clergy to lose sight of the spiritual aspect of their lives when the details of running a parish or everyday living demand attention. Talking about this facet of their lives has helped the clergy and spouses focus on what might be done to stay spiritually nourished. Spiritual growth can be addressed as a solitary and a corporate activity. Several approaches have been considered by dioceses, including the development of a list of spiritual directors in the region. Overnight retreats for clergy and/or spouses are proposed within dioceses that do not have them on a regular basis. Bible study has both personal and corporate value. One diocesan proposal is that clergy and spouses gather regionally for regular Bible study and prayer.

As prayer is the language of faith, committees have explored ways to give intercessory prayer even more meaning in their lives as a community. Several dioceses suggest prayer calendars or covenants which would allow clergy and spouses to pray for each other specifically in times of crisis and on a regular cycle.

Other Concerns

When any committee looks at tangible resources for clergy and their spouses, the initial inclination might be to focus on the needs of the majority of clergy, those that are white, male, and married. If relationships are important to the overall health of clergy, then certainly supporting healthy marriages is also important. At the same time, dioceses are aware that there are clergy in the diocese who are not white, male, or married. In some cases, those who are not married are gay. Gay and lesbian clergy often feel (and are) excluded from the life of a diocese. As the data brought out, many of the people answering the questionnaire also are not sure about the extent to which people of color and single clergy feel included. A possible step seen by many of the committees is to reach a better understanding of what being *inclusive* might involve for the diocese and how better to understand the situations of those not in the majority.

Finally

The Clergy/Family Project has provided a wealth of information about positive and negative contributors to the overall health of clergy and clergy spouses. Serious problems frequently are the ones that are most visible, create the most pain, and receive the most attention. Clearly, these problems must be addressed. There are ways of accomplishing that. In the meantime, the data show that when clergy and spouses feel healthy and energetic, are not lonely and isolated, feel they are growing spiritually, and feel joy and satisfaction in their work in the church, they are healthy people. The key to creating an environment in which this can happen lies in knowing what their particular issues and concerns are, knowing their circumstances and situations, knowing what they believe would be helpful, knowing what resources would best meet their needs and be utilized, and making them a part of what happens. Knowledge forms the basis for informed action.

Notes

CHAPTER ONE

1. Thomas Maeder, "Wounded Healers," *The Atlantic Monthly* (January 1989): 37. Maeder contends that "helping professions" such as ministry and psychotherapy often attract emotionally unstable individuals. Whether the factors contributing to the instability have been adequately resolved or sealed off has direct bearing on their capacity to help others. The concept of the wounded healer is discussed further in Chapter II.

2. H. Newton Malony and Richard A. Hunt, *The Psychology of Clergy* (Harrisburg: Morehouse Publishing, 1991), p. 2. Malony and Hunt present Brooks Holifield's historical stereotypes of the ideal minister as reflective of society's image of the cultural hero: the common man plus gentleman (frontier days); the man of power-visionary (post-Civil War); the social reformer (end of the nineteenth century); the manager (post-World War I).

3. Urban T. Holmes III, *The Priest in Community: Exploring the Roots of Ministry* (New York: The Seabury Press, 1978), p. 10.

4. Edwin H. Friedman, *Generation to Generation: Family Process in Church and Synagogue.* (New York: Guilford Press, 1985), pp. 278–279. In the language of family systems theory, Friedman would contend that "emotional process operates the same way in all families" and that the idea that clergy families are different is a myth. This is not meant to deny that there may be some factors/expectations peculiar to the ministry. But clergy and their families are no different from others in the way in which they are affected by what happens to them.

5. The Clergy Family Project process begins with the gathering of anecdotal data. Making use of the biblical tradition of storytelling, a committee representative of the diocese begins by talking about personal encounters with the church and faith and exploring the history of the diocese. Through this method common themes emerge, and connections are made. The committee then distributes a questionnaire to clergy and spouses of their diocese.

When the responses are all in, the committee gathers to study the compiled data, again looking at common themes, at strengths and needs. Building on the discussions and the data, members begin to explore resources their diocese might institute to address the needs expressed.

The process used by the project is outlined in *The Manual for Clergy/ Family Committees*. An aim of the project is to make clergy and spouses active participants in examining their strengths and needs and developing resources rather than being merely subject to the diagnosis and prescription of someone outside their system. Critical to the project's thinking is that any action based on what a diocese discerns for itself, about itself, is apt to be more relevant to the needs of the diocese and owned by it.

6. The Episcopal dioceses of Atlanta, Central New York, Hawaii, Iowa, Kansas, Lexington, Louisville, Missouri, Northern Indiana, Oregon, Southern Ohio, and Western North Carolina are the sources of the present data.

CHAPTER TWO

7. Karl Menninger, *The Vital Balance: The Life Process in Mental Health and Illness* (New York: The Viking Press, 1963), p. 134. The balance Menninger is referring to is the interaction between a person's internal and external environment. A "vital balance" is being able to handle stress effectively. A person with a relatively healthy and intact ego will have "established a system of relationships with love objects, a network of intercommunication, a program of life involving work satisfactions and play satisfactions, . . . learned to channel his aggressiveness in the least harmful directions and toward the most suitable objects, . . . found ways to be creative within the limits of his talents, . . . developed a love-and-let-love attitude toward the universe."

8. *Menninger Perspective* No. 4 (1988): 14. This is the quarterly of the Menninger Foundation.

9. Michael E. Kerr and Murray Bowen, *Family Evaluation* (New York: W. W. Norton, 1988), p. 333. The eight concepts are: scale of differentiation, triangles, nuclear family emotional process, family projection process, multigenerational transmission process, sibling position, emotional cutoff, and societal emotional process.

10. Friedman, *Generation to Generation*, p. 27.

11. Lloyd Retiger, *Coping with Clergy Burnout* (Valley Forge, Pa.: Judson Press, 1981), pp. 100–105 et passim. Social health is subsumed in Retiger's typology under "mental" self-awareness and support, which entails develop-

ing supportive intimate relationship with others as well as getting assistance in clergy support groups.

12. Henri J. M. Nouwen, "Reborn from Above," *Spiritual Life* (Spring 1992): 29. Quarterly of the Washington province of Discalced Carmelite Friars, Inc., Washington D.C. Nouwen is quoting Thomas Phillippe.

13. Ibid., p. 30.

14. Henri J. M. Nouwen, *The Wounded Healer* (New York: Image Book, Doubleday, 1979), p. 92. Nouwen reminds us it may be a good thing that perfection is not attainable because of the need to be able to share our weakness and loneliness with others. What is important is that "the minister who has come to terms with his own loneliness and is at home in his own house is a host who offers hospitality to his guests."

15. Ibid., p. 82. Nouwen's "wounded healer" is not quite analogous to Maeder's wounded healer described in Chapter One. Maeder applies the term equally to describe effective and ineffective "care givers" but stresses the need to heal one's own wounds in order to be helpful to others. That is in keeping with Nouwen's "wounded healer."

16. Roberta C. Bondi, *To Pray and to Love: Conversations on Prayer with the Early Church* (Minneapolis: Fortress Press, 1991), pp. 76–82.

17. The fishbowl "private" life of pastors and their spouses and children which arises out of the likelihood that they are more closely watched and held to higher behavioral expectations by parishioners and others in the community—thus, causing stress—is a recurrent theme in the following books and articles:

Gilbert, Barbara G. *Who Ministers to Ministers? A Study of Support Systems for Clergy and Spouses.* Washington: The Alban Institute, 1987.

Lee, Cameron and Jack Balswick. *Life in a Glass House: The Minister's Family in Its Unique Social Context.* Grand Rapids: Ministry Resources Library, Zondervan Publishing House, 1989.

Mace, David and Vera Mace. *What's Happening to Clergy Marriages.* Nashville: Abingdon Press, 1980.

Marciano, Teresa. "Corporate Church, Ministry and Ministerial Family: Embedded Employment and Measures of Success." *Marriage and Family Review* 15: 171–193.

Norell, Elizabeth J. "Clergy Family Satisfaction: A Review." *Family Science Review* 4 (1989): 69–93.

Richmond, Lee, Carole Rayburn, and Lynn Roger. "Clergymen, Clergy-

women and Their Spouses: Stress in Professional Religious Families."
Journal of Career Development 12 (September 1985): 81–85.

Warner, Janelle and John D. Carter. "Loneliness, Marital Adjustment
and Burnout in Pastoral and Lay Persons." *Journal of Psychology and Theology*
12 (1984): 125–131.

18. Overall Health Scores of Clergy and Spouses

	Very Healthy (scores 4, 5)	Fair to Unhealthy (scores 10–16)
Pastors	30%	19%
Their Spouses	27%	28%
Clergy, not parish	34%	17%
Their Spouses	24%	28%
Retired Clergy	43%	7%
Their Spouses	42%	13%

19. How Often Activity Done In an Average Week

	Rarely, Never	Four or More Times
1. Exercised for 15–20 minutes at one stretch		
pastors	21%	34%
and spouses	21	33
non-parochial clergy	23	39
and spouses	19	32
retired clergy	16	47
and spouses	18	44
2. Spent 1–2 hours alone with spouse (or *if* not married) close friend		
pastors	5%	56%
and spouses	4	58
non-parochial clergy	3	68
and spouses	7	73
retired clergy	2	76
and spouses	2	81

3. Had a meal and/or went to
   a recreational or cultural
   event with friends

pastors	25%	17%
and spouses	30	16
non-parochial clergy	19	21
and spouses	28	16
retired clergy	17	23
and spouses	20	21

4. Spent an hour or two alone
   —reflecting, reading,
   hobbies, etc.

pastors	5%	50%
and spouses	10	45
non-parochial clergy	4	58
and spouses	10	56
retired clergy	0	75
and spouses	4	68

5. Spent 15 minutes or more in
   personal prayer, meditation

pastors	4%	71%
and spouses	21	41
non-parochial clergy	3	66
and spouses	24	49
retired clergy	2	85
and spouses	12	56

20. Correlations for the total sample of active clergy and their spouses with their scores on the overall health index and the amount of time they spent in various activities mentioned are all significant at the .001 level: overall health (good to poor) and amount time (none to much) spent in: physical exercise $-.12$; with spouse or close friend $-.26$; socializing with friends $-.19$; alone in hobbies $-.17$; and in private prayer and meditation $-.22$.

CHAPTER THREE
21. The impact of being reared in dysfunctional families, particularly for clergy, is laid out clearly for readers by Edwin Friedman, *Generation to*

Generation: Family Process in Church and Synagogue (New York: Guilford Press, 1988).

22. Hank Whittemore, "Ministers Under Stress," *Parade Magazine* (April 14, 1991): 20-21. As indicated in Chapter One, these stories are fairly prevalent about clergy in all denominations.

23. Friedman, cited above, states at the outset (p. 19) a point he makes throughout his book, *Generation to Generation*, that "the family member with the obvious symptom is to be seen not as the 'sick one' but as the one in whom the family's stress or pathology has surfaced."

24. In most cases, participating dioceses elected to use an identification number for each clergy and spouse to whom they sent a survey so that they could follow up on non-returns. The diocese was given a list of all identification numbers received at Hartford Seminary. The seminary was not given the names of clergy or spouses that matched the identification numbers. The completed questionnaires came back directly to Hartford Seminary for data processing and were destroyed after information was abstracted. The diocese never saw any of the completed questionnaires.

25. The term "nuclear" is used throughout to denote the family with whom clergy presently live.

26. Retiger in *Coping with Clergy Burnout*, cited in Chapter Two, has several chapters in which the symptoms of beginning and advanced burnout are fairly dramatically described.

27. Clergy sexual "abuse" of parishioners may range from affairs with parishioners to sexual fondling of children, the latter of course being particularly heinous. In either instance, pastors may be removed from their position. Pastor-parishioners sexual relationships are a violation of professional trust and—as seen in Catholic, Lutheran, Methodist, Presbyterian, United Church of Christ as well as Episcopal denominational circles—a matter of much debate and legal suits against the judicatories of the offending cleric. For example only, see the series "Clergy Sexual Abuse" starting in the September 1991 issue of *Episcopal Life*, the national Episcopal newsletter; Linda Majka, *Sexual Harassment in the United Methodist Church* (Dayton, Ohio: General Council on Ministries, United Methodist Church, 1990); Karen Lebacqz and Ronald Burton, *Sex in the Parish* (Louisville: Westminster/John Knox, 1991).

28. Of course, it is theoretically possible, for example, that Pastor A. who can name five severe problems in his family currently is more "aware" of real

difficulties than Pastor B. who reports no severe problems but is actually in a more dysfunctional family—because Pastor B. is in a state of "denial." However, the analysis here has to proceed on the assumption that those who recognize several problems present in their families are indeed seeing their families as more dysfunctional than those who do not have or recognize they have family problems of such magnitude.

29. For example, the correlation between the number of problems in the families of pastors when they were growing up and the number of problems these same pastors report in their own families now is .37 and for their spouses, .39. Both of these correlations are significant at the .001 levels

30. The correlations just for parochial clergy and spouses (which are very similar to those for active non-parochial) are as follows:

Parish Clergy and Spouses
Overall Health Index
(low scores–very healthy to high scores–very unhealthy):

	Clergy	Spouses
Correlation with:		
Total Number of Problems in Family as a Child	.14**	.19**
Total Number of Problems in Family Now	.35**	.36**

** = significant at .001 level

31. To test this hypothesis, mean scores on the Overall Health Index were calculated as a result of number of present serious problems in the family, controlling for number of serious problems in the family of origin. The importance of number of serious problems now, and the relative unimportance of problems growing up, are illustrated in the following table for

All Active Clergy (N=667)
Scores on Overall Health Index

Family Now: Problem Free main mean score . 6.1
Growing Up: problem free 6.2
                3+ problems . . . 6.3

Family Now: One Problem 7.0
              Growing Up: problem free 6.9
                            3+ problems   . . . 7.4

Family Now: Two Problems 7.6
              Growing Up: problem free 7.3
                            3+ problems   . . . 7.8

Family Now: Three+ Problems 8.7
              Growing Up: problem free 8.2
                            3+ problems   . . . 8.8

32. This rate of currently divorced clergy compares favorably with that of 10 percent of Protestant laity who are currently divorced, as estimated by Wade Clark Roof and William McKinney, *American Mainline Religion: Its Changing Shape and Future* (New Brunswick, N.J.: Rutgers University Press, 1987), p. 156. It is more difficult to compare divorce statistics accurately than we had anticipated—in part due to the fact that some authors unwittingly compare rate of "now divorced" in one population to "ever divorced" in the same or another population. Still others calculate divorce rate on percent of those who are married over age 15, while others calculate the rate based on percent of adults single and married in the population.

33.
Divorce Statistics (1991–92 data only)

a) **Now divorced**

               % all clergy 6.8% (men 4.7%, women 16.0%)
  Parochial clergy   6.6% (men 3.9%, women 19.5%)
  Non-parochial clergy   5.8% (men 6.3%, women 3.6%)
  Retired clergy   3.6% (men 3.9%, women 0%)
  Deacons   16.0% (men 11.1%, women 20.5%)

b) **Ever divorced** (includes remarriage)

               % all clergy 24.9% (men 24.3%, women 26.9%)
  Parochial clergy   27.1% (men 26.0%, women 31.7%)
  Non-parochial clergy   28.6% (men 30.1%, women 23.5%)
  Retired clergy   11.9% (men 13.8%, women 3.4%)
  Deacons   29.6% (men 25.0%, women 33.3%)

c) Now and ever divorced by year of ordination and gender (all clergy)
bold % = now divorced
Italic % = ever divorced
Percentages are of N (number ordained in those years)

Year of ordination	MEN	WOMEN
1987–92	**7%**	**42%**
	30% (N 54)	*47% (N 31)*
1983–86	**6%**	**26%**
	29% (N 49)	*44% (N 46)*
1973–82	**6%**	**36%**
	26% (N 133)	*32% (N 25)*
1963–72	**3%** (N 199)	**0**
		28% (5 deacons)
Up to 1992	**5%**	
	19% (N 226)	

d) **Parochial clergy** *only* (ordained in the last ten years)
   % = ever divorced (by age)

Forty and under	15% (N 39)
41 to 50 years old	33% (N 54)
51 to 60 years old	71% (N 14)
Over 60 years old	43% (N 23)

e) In a 1993–1994 survey of ordained women and men in fifteen denominations, of the 233 Episcopal clergywomen participating in that study, 30 percent have ever been divorced and of the 191 clergymen 25 percent have ever been divorced. Barbara Brown Zikmund, Adair T. Lummis, and Patricia M. Y. Chang, *An Uphill Calling: Ordained Women and Men in the Contemporary Protestant Church* (Louisville: Westminister/John Knox, 1997).

34. Karl Menninger, *The Vital Balance: The Life Process in Mental Health and Illness* (New York: The Viking Press, 1963), Chapter XVI.

CHAPTER FOUR
35. Paul Mickey and Ginny W. Ashmore, *Clergy Families: Is Normal Life Possible?* (Grand Rapids: Zondervan Publishing House, 1991), pp. 66–67.

"Twenty-five years ago the organic-unity model of ministry encouraged pastors to assume that family and occupation were the same thing," as Mickey and Ashmore describe the situation. In comparison, these authors see the ministry today as very much more fragmented due to the complexity of society and cross-pressures on the church and pastor.

36. Jackson W. Carroll, *As One with Authority* (Louisville: Westminster/John Knox Press, 1991), p. 22. Carroll discusses this contemporary phenomenon of laity refusing to accept the "faith as if it were a whole cloth," but rather selecting out those parts which appeal, creating problems for clergy religious authority.

37. Paula Nesbitt, "Lamentations: The Politics of Gender and Ministry" (Washington: Paper presented at the Society for the Scientific Study of Religion, November, 1992). Nesbitt reviews literature on the decline in the number of young men for the ministry and its interpretation by denominational offices and others as symbolic of decline of ministry as an occupation. She presents data for Unitarians and Episcopalians.

38. The challenge by laity to the religious authority of the clergy, and stronger lay criticism of the way pastors attempted to fulfill all roles demanded of them—for most of which they had little training—are sagas found in: David R. Covell Jr., *Who Do Men Say That I Am?* (Strategic Research Services Group, Executive Council of the Episcopal Church, 1970); Yoshio Fukuyama, *The Ministry in Transition* (University Park, Pa.: The Penn State University Press, 1972); Jeffrey K. Hadden, *The Gathering Storm in Churches* (Garden City, N.Y.: Doubleday, 1969); Gerald J. Jud, Edgar W. Mills Jr., Genevieve Walters Burch, *Ex-Pastors: Why Men Leave the Parish Ministry* (Philadelphia: Pilgrim Press, 1970); Donald P. Smith, *Clergy in the Crossfire* (Philadelphia: The Westminster Press, 1972).

39. Cited in H. Newton Malony and Richard A. Hunt, *The Psychology of Clergy* (Harrisburg: Morehouse-Barlow, 1991), p. 2. Holifield puts forth a progression of clergy images over the last 150 years from a combination of "common man" and gentleman to visionary to liberal/progressive to manager. Though such a progression might well be seen as reflective of the majority—white and male—at the same time it fits in with an evolution in the profession.

40. Teresa Marciano, "Corporate Church, Ministry, and Ministerial Family: Embedded Employment and Measures of Success," *Marriage and Family Review* 15 (1990): 171–193. Marciano makes a strong argument for

the ministry being the most "embedded employment" in the sense that work and private life are normatively supposed to be of one piece and attributes this in major part to the divine call clergy are also normatively supposed to have for the ministry.

41. Christopher Jencks and David Riesman, *The Academic Revolution* (Garden City, N.Y.: Doubleday, 1968), pp. 209–211, 254 et passim. Like other occupations by the fifties, the ordained ministry could not afford to ignore the "academic revolution" or the professionalization of vocations which required graduate level degrees of its practitioners. Being a graduate specialty, as Jencks and Riesman explain, "enhances the status of the program and those who teach in it, and also makes the profession as a whole more exclusive and more prestigious" (p. 254). Therefore, denominations and seminaries pressed for having education for ministry become distinctly "a graduate specialty." The fifties and sixties witnessed the establishment of university-affiliated, university-like seminaries, which required a four-year college degree for entrance, and began to offer degrees beyond the B.D.-M.Div. This trend extended even to historic denominational seminaries.

The proliferation of D.Min. programs in the seventies to the present for those who are already pastors gives further evidence that the "professionalization" of ministry by requiring higher levels of formal education is continuing.

Other characteristics distinguishing a "profession"—such as the development of expertise in a specialized area and common standards for clergy which could be employed for ordination, hiring, and promotion—were argued in the late sixties in a book which received much heated debate when it was first published but would be quite acceptable to most now—James D. Glasse, *Profession: Minister* (Nashville: Abingdon, 1968).

42. Everett Hughes and A. DeBaggis, "Systems of Theological Education in the United States," in E. Hughes et. al., *Education for the Professions of Medicine, Law, Theology and Social Welfare* (New York: Carnegie Commission, 1973), pp. 169–200. In the early seventies Hughes proclaimed: "Divinity, once the Queen of Professions, is in a parlous state" (pp. 2–3), and he and DeBaggis went on to describe how the many different denominations, each with its own seminary, made it difficult to establish common standards of what a B.D.-M.Div. prepared clergy to do as practitioners. This situation was (and is!) exacerbated by disagreement among faculty within seminaries over what future clergy should be learning.

43. See endnote 17 in Chapter Two.

44. Friedman, *Generation to Generation*, p. 278.

45. Percentage equals percentage who *strongly agree* Clergy Families Do Face Different Pressures than Families of Secular Professionals

Pastors	57%
Their Spouses	69%
Clergy, Not Parish	56%
Their Spouses	60%
Retired Clergy	54%
Their Spouses	69%

46. Friedman would say that what counts is the capacity to differentiate and at the same time stay in relationship with others. Friedman does agree that there is a strong "emotional interlock" between work and family for clergy. He might also agree that the "organic-unity" model of ministry increases the difficulty clergy might have in clearly defining how much time they should give to the parish and how much time (and when) to their families, friends, and selves. Friedman warns, however, that holding to a perception clergy families are "different" and "special" can potentially be destructive to their well-being. Though the setting and some of the circumstances may be different, clergy have the same life experiences to cope with and the same problems in relationship that anyone else has; they rely on the same techniques others do to cope with their anxieties; and they are equally bound to understand their responses and behaviors.

47. Friedman contends that holding to the "myth" that clergy families are "different" keeps clergy family members from examining their relationships with each other and the congregation as systems over which they can exert some influence and taking responsibility for stresses and problems afflicting the family (pp. 281-282). He states: "For clergy more than for any other professionals, work and family systems plug all too easily into one another and significant changes in either system may be quicker to unbalance the other. Yet even that difference does not really make the clergy family 'different.' Rather, it means that in order to ensure its overall family health, differentiation of self is more imperative" (p. 279).

48. Numbers = mean scores on Overall Health Index (low scores = very healthy, high scores = unhealthy)

	Parish		Non-Parish		Retired	
	Pr	Sp	Pr	Sp	Pr	Sp
Clergy Families are Different						
Strongly Agree	7.6	8.3	7.1	8.4	6.5	6.0
Somewhat Agree to Disagree	6.7	6.6	6.7	7.3	5.6	7.1

49. The statistical correlation between pastors and spouses seeing the clergy family as different and believing the church is responsible for the well-being of clergy families is .32 for pastors and .44 for spouses, significant at the .001 level.

50. Holmes, *The Priest in Community*, p. 8.

51. The Book of Common Prayer, (New York: Church Pension Fund, 1979), p. 532.

52. Several of the items were reversed in the questionnaire. For the sake of the reader, the verb clauses have been edited for consistency, i.e., each can be answered with a "yes."

53. The alphas of scale reliability for the Ability to Differentiate Scale are .77 for parish clergy and .79 for their spouses. Possible scores range from 7 to 29.

54. The correlations between number of problems in the clergy family (0 to 13) and ability to set boundaries (poor to good) is: −.25 for pastors and −.42 for their spouses, significant at the .001 level.

55. Among active clergy and spouses, correlations (significant at .001 level) with amount of time per week spent with a spouse or significant other and degree of satisfaction with one's marriage are −.31 for priests and −.30 for spouses.

Correlations with amount of time spent in social/recreational activities with friends and degree of satisfaction with one's social life are: −.27 for priests and −.34 for spouses.

56. Statistically significant correlations (.001 level) between having a satisfying social life and believing clergy families are "special" (−.27 for pastors and −.18 for spouses); being in a functional-dysfunctional family (.34 for pastors and spouses); having poor to excellent abilities in maintaining the

boundary between church and home (–.41 for pastors, –.46 for spouses); and having good overall health (.52 for pastors, .57 for spouses).

57. Numbers = mean scores on Overall Health Index (low scores = very healthy, high scores = unhealthy)

Social Life	Parish		Non-Parish		Retired	
	Pr	Sp	Pr	Sp	Pr	Sp
Very Satisfactory	5.3	5.7	5.7	6.1	5.5	5.6
Quite Satisfactory	6.8	7.3	6.6	8.1	6.4	6.3
Unsatisfactory	8.9	9.8	8.9	9.7	7.9	8.1

CHAPTER FIVE

58. The other items in this section are: organizing and motivating paid staff and volunteers to do the work of the church, presiding at meetings of large groups, teaching children, and working with teens.

59. The statistical correlations between pastor self-ratings as being effective in stimulating laity to outreach ministry and the characteristic of the congregation named are between .14 and .28, significant at the .001 level.

60. The correlation between wealth of the congregation and the pastor's effectiveness self-rating in meeting the church budget is a strong correlation of .42, significant at the .001 level or higher.

61. The correlation between effectiveness in pastoral counseling and being in a dysfunctional family is only –.11, significant at the .01 level. But it is in the direction of showing that the more problems the pastor has, the more apt s/he is to counsel others effectively. (There was no relationship between overall health of clergy and their perceived effectiveness in pastoral counseling.)

62. Maeder, "Wounded Healers."

63. The importance of a good professional self-concept in handling stress and particularly in commitment to the profession is a focal discussion in empirical studies of the parish ministry by Jud, Mills, and Burch, *Ex-Pastors*; for professional musicians by Charles Kadushin, "The Professional Self-Concept of Music Students," *American Journal of Sociology* 75 (1969): 389–404; and for those who will be lawyers by Wagner Thielens, "The Occupational Self-Image of the Law Student," paper presented at the American Sociological Association national meeting (1963).

64. The alpha reliability is .62 for the Professional Self-Concept scale, with scores ranging from 4 (low) to 16 (high).

65. Jud, Mills, and Burch, in *Ex-Pastors*, did not actually measure professional self-concept but used this as a theoretical construct to explain a major reason why clergy left this vocation. In this present study there is a strong correlation between professional self-concept (low to high) and giving serious consideration to leaving the parish ministry (usually to never) of .46, significant at the .001 level or higher.

66. Correlations (all significant at the .001 level) between professional self-concept (weak to strong) and:
- financial health of the congregations (excellent ... in serious difficulty) –.31
- membership (growing to declining) –.26
- number of parishioners at Sunday morning service .18
- lay involvement (most inactive to a majority active in church other than Sunday morning) .37.

67. The correlations (significant at .001 level) between professional self-concept (low to high) for pastors and:
- amount of church salary (low to high) .17
- can live comfortably on income (usually true to usually false) –.36.

68. Julie A. Wortman, "High Hurdles Confront Those Seeking Ordination," *Episcopal Life* (September 1991): 10.

69. The correlation for pastors between having a working spouse and their total family income (low to high) is –.33, significant at .001 level. The correlation for pastors between total family income and feeling able to live comfortably on income is –.32, significant at .001 level.

70. Correlation between pastors' professional self-concept and:
- feeling supported by the bishop is –.22
- feeling free to call the bishop rather than waiting for the bishop to call is –.17
- and believing the bishop knows the pastor well as "a person" is –.17, all correlations significant at .001 level.

71. Correlation between pastors' professional self-concepts and.
- feeling well supported by "other Episcopal clergy in this diocese" is .18, significant at .001 level
- feeling well supported by "most of the clergy pastoring Churches of other denominations in my community" is –.11, significant at the .01 level.

72. The relationship between clergy self-esteem or professional self-

concept and obtaining support from other clergy is found and discussed by Gilbert and by Mills. Barbara G. Gilbert, *Who Ministers to Ministers? A Study of Support Systems for Clergy and Spouses* (Washington: the Alban Institute, 1987), pp. 45–47 et passim; Edgar W. Mills Jr., "Review of Recent Social Science Research on Stress" in Loren B. Mead, Barry Evans, Edgar W. Mills Jr., and Clement W. Welsh, *Personal and Professional Needs of the Clergy of the Episcopal Church* (New York: The Episcopal Church Foundation, 1988), pp. 38–67.

CHAPTER SIX

73. Statistics about the growth of women clergy in all denominations can be found in Constant Jacquet Jr., *Women Ministers in 1986 and 1977: a Ten Year View* (National Council of Churches, 1988); and yearly reports on enrollment statistics from the Association of Accredited Seminaries (Vandalia, Ohio).

74. Seminarians in all mainline Protestant denominations and ecumenical seminaries tend to be "thirty-something," with Episcopalians of both genders tending to be about thirty-five. Ellis Larsen and James M. Shopshire, "A Profile of Contemporary Seminarians," *Theological Education* 24 (Spring 1988), entire issue.

75. In 1980, 55 percent of the women to 94 percent of the men who are pastors of churches in mainline Protestant denominations overall were married. Jackson W. Carroll, Barbara Hargrove, and Adair T. Lummis, *Women of the Cloth* (San Francisco: Harper and Row, 1983), p. 251.

76. Zikmund, Lummis, and Chang, *Uphill Calling*. Among clergy surveyed in the 1993–1994 interdenominational study, 62 percent of the women and 92 percent of the men are married.

77. Larsen and Shopshire, "Contemporary Seminarians," pp. 27–28.

78. George Judson, "Congregation Confronts a Changing Ministry," *The New York Times*, July 19–20, 1992, p. 1.

79. Among the newly ordained Episcopal clergy nationwide in 1986, 22 out of 57 women responding were single, and of these single women, 77 percent had children at home. Adair T. Lummis, "Minister, Debtor and Mother," paper read at the Society for the Scientific Study of Religious Research—Religious Research Association annual meetings, Louisville (October 1987).

80. A study done in the late seventies of black Episcopal seminarians and

clergy indicated that there were few black students in seminaries and that black clergy in dioceses were not actively recruiting potential black clergy— in part because they themselves were dissatisfied with opportunities for the career advancement in the church enjoyed by white clergy. Franklin D. Turner and Adair T. Lummis, "Black Clergy in the Episcopal Church: Recruitment, Training, and Deployment" (Office for Black Ministries, Episcopal Church Center, 1979).

81. For example, Nesbitt reports that 83 percent of men compared to 57 percent of the women, regardless of marital status, had full-time entry level positions among the 1985 new priests. Paula D. Nesbitt, "Clergy Feminization: Controlled Labor or Liberationist Change?", paper presented at the annual meetings of the Association for the Sociology of Religion, Cincinnati (August 1991).

82. Over half of the women (55 percent) compared to fewer men (36 percent) in non-parochial clergy positions themselves—agreed that clergy in "alternate ministries" are accorded less recognition than parish clergy in their dioceses.

83. Among active clergy in this study the amount of salary actually received is a major factor in whether they feel adequately compensated, as well as whether the salary they have now is about what they had expected to receive (or better) on ordination. Both men and women clergy earning a cash salary of under $20,000 believe they are underpaid as compared to those who earn over $25,000. The more recently ordained clergy agree they are getting about what they expected but still are more apt than those ordained for some years to feel insufficiently compensated—due mainly to their relatively low salaries.

84. Two-fifths of the pastors in the study by Mickey and Ashmore, *Clergy Families*, believed that low salary is a major source of stress in their families (p. 113).

85. The correlation between time spent in private prayer per week (few to many times) and overall health (good to poor) is for clergywomen –.35 but for clergymen only –.13, both correlations significant at the .001 level.

CHAPTER SEVEN

86. Anne Llewellyn Barstow, "The First Generations of Anglican Clergy Wives: Heroines or Whores?", *Historical Magazine of the Protestant Episcopal Church* (March 1983): 3. Barstow surveys the perilous path that clergy wives

took during the Reformation from a point in which their lives were in danger to one in which they emerge as conventional models of women in a male-dominated culture. Our thanks to Mary Donovan, historian, for bringing this article to our attention.

87. Jasper Ridley, *Thomas Cranmer* (Oxford: Clarendon Press, 1962), pp. 147–151.

88. Barstow, "Heroines or Whores?," p. 14.

89. In the 1979 national survey of clergy in eight denominations two-thirds of the married clergywomen were married to an ordained person, compared to less than 3 percent of the married clergymen. Most of the clergy couples at that time wanted to work, and were working, in the same parish; but around a third had to be in different congregations. Other aspects of the deployment picture of clergy couples in 1980 are also described in: Jackson Carroll, Barbara Hargrove, and Adair T. Lummis, *Women of the Cloth: A New Opportunity for Churches* (San Francisco: Harper and Row, 1983), pp. 135–147.

The book by E. M. Rallings and David J. Pratto, *Two-Clergy Marriages: A Special Case of Dual Careers* (Lantham, Md.: University Press of America, 1984) focuses on the career and life style issues attendant on being part of a clergy couple.

90. Carroll et al., *Women of the Cloth*, p. 135.

91. Ibid., p. 193.

92. Personal communication with Odessa Elliott, December 17, 1992.

93. In the now classic cross-denominational study by Mace and Mace, these authors found that wives were twice as concerned about money-management being a problem as were their ordained husbands. David Mace and Vera Mace, *What's Happening to Clergy Marriages* (Nashville: Abingdon Press, 1980), p. 40. A similar finding was reported in a study of UCC clergy by Barbara G. Gilbert, *Who Ministers to Ministers? A Study of Support Systems for Clergy and Spouses* (Washington: The Alban Institute, 1987), pp. 10–11.

Using various sources, but principally graduates and their spouses from Fuller Seminary, Lee and Balswick suggest that a major stress for clergy wives—not having enough money—is more noticed by wives than by their clergy husbands since it falls to the wife to manage household finances and search for outside employment if the pastor's salary is insufficient. Cameron Lee and Jack Balswick, *Life in a Glass House: The Minister's Family in Its Unique*

Social Context (Grand Rapids: Zondervan Publishing Company, 1989), pp. 192–194.

94. The correlation between number of family problems (0 to 13) and perception of being able to live comfortably on family income for husbands of clergywomen is not significant; for wives of clergymen it is .32, significant at the .001 level.

95. In illustration, in relatively impoverished married clergy families, with total incomes under $30,000—44 percent of the men to 39 percent of the women spouses of clergy said their working was "very important" for family finances. Whereas in relatively well-to-do married clergy families, with total incomes of $65,000 and over, 88 percent of the men to 56 percent of the women spouses of clergy said their own salaries are "very important" in their families' financial security.

96. Among spouses, holding a secular job is correlated .45 with the importance of contributing to family financial security and .27 with wanting a career of one's own.

97. Greenbacker and Taylor, for example, comment: "Why do ministers' wives work? For money, certainly. But also for their own sense of service, their searches for self and their searches for friends" (pp. 134–135). In this study of clergy wives, over three-fourths of whom were employed, the modal group—24 percent—said they went back to work for financial and professional reasons (pp. 120–124). Liz Greenbacker and Sherry Taylor, *Private Lives of Ministers' Wives* (Far Hills, N.J.: New Horizons Press, 1991).

98. William Douglas, *Ministers' Wives* (New York: Harper and Row, 1965) pp. 33–43, especially, cited in Charles William Stewart, *Person and Profession: Career Development in Ministry* (Nashville: Abingdon Press, 1974), pp. 100–102, who also expands the typology to include the newest type of clergy wife—the working wife.

99. These authors, on the basis of interviews, suggest that clergy wives have an easier time with boundary maintenance if they have their own careers. Greenbacker and Taylor, *Private Lives*, p. 123.

100. Lee and Balswick, *Life in a Glass House*, p. 159.

101. Men married to women pastors appear to have "more freedom not to participate" in their wives' congregations than would still be the case with most wives of clergymen, although the authors suggest this difference may diminish in strength "as women move away from the historical role of 'minister's wife'." Clearly, however, husbands of clergy are better able on the

average to "differentiate" themselves from the congregations than wives of clergy. Laura Deming and Jack Stubbs, *Men Married to Ministers* (Washington: Alban Institute, 1986), pp. 12–13, 18–19.

102. Odessa Elliott, personal communication, December 17, 1992, found through informal group interviews using ECUNET with husbands of women pastors that although the "men said they had very carefully stayed 'uninvolved' (in the congregations their wives pastored), . . . they found they had as much difficulty in 'saying good-by' as their wives" did on moving to take a new parish position.

103. In their study of clergy wives, Greenbacker and Taylor found that 29 percent make most of their friends within their congregation, 42 percent both inside and outside the church, and 21 percent more exclusively outside the church. *Private Lives*, p. 155.

For both clergy and spouses, Mickey and Ashmore's findings indicate that one of the great advantages of the parish is the personal support and good friends husband and wife can make within their congregation. *Clergy Families*, pp. 138–139.

CHAPTER EIGHT

104. Diocese of Missouri, Proposal for a Diocesan Pastoral Care Program, July 20, 1992. This proposal presented to the Diocesan Convention, January 1993.

Questions for Discussion

The following series of questions are keyed to each chapter. Other questions may come to mind for you. Any of these questions would be suitable for individual reflection, discussion with your spouse, spouse groups, clergy groups, or groups made up of clergy and lay people. You may also think of other configurations.

Chapter One

Whether you are ordained or married to a priest or a lay person, how would you describe your ministry? What have been the challenges you have faced, and what have been the blessings?

Do you think clergy are different, or clergy families different from others? What makes you think that?

In reflecting on your experience in the church, in what way/s has it been good and in what way/s problematic?

What stereotypes do you think exist about clergy or spouses? To what extent do you find them accurate or inaccurate?

As a lay person, as a priest, or as a spouse: In what ways are your circumstances similar to those of other people in the parish and community? And, as a lay person, how are your circumstances similar to your parish priest or his/her spouse?

Chapter Two

How would you describe an emotionally healthy person? A spiritually healthy person? What do you do to stay healthy?

How does Nouwen's description of the wounded healer fit with your experience?

Do you believe that parishes collude with the self-sacrifice image of clergy? In what way? If you agree, how might you change this?

Looking at the health index on page 18, how would you respond to those statements?

If you are a lay person: How well does the Health Index describe you? How do you work with your priest to support what he/she needs to stay healthy?

Chapter Three

What do you think about the suggestion that clergy may be attracted to the ordained ministry by "unresolved problems in their own childhood"? Were there any problems in the family in which you grew up? How were they dealt with?

What are the emotional hurdles you have leapt, and how have you transcended them? Does anyone in your family now have a severe problem? How does that affect you, your family, or your work? Where have you found help?

How would you explain the finding that retired clergy and spouses apparently have fewer problems?

Chapter Four

What demands does your work place put on you? How do you manage them?

Do you see any tension in your life between your vocational demands and personal life? How do you balance them?

What do you think are the challenges to the ordained ministry today? Are things different now from when you started out?

Is your profession what you thought it would be when you began? If not, what changes have occurred?

Would you agree that clergy families face some different pressures as a family than do those families of professionals in secular employ? What might the disadvantages of such thinking be?

Being able to maintain satisfactory boundaries between the church and private life is a challenge for many clergy and spouses. In what ways do you find maintaining boundaries difficult for you? How do you manage the challenge?

Chapter Five

The areas of competency listed in the questionnaire are: preaching, planning and leading worship, meeting the church budget, crisis ministry, pastoral counseling, visiting sick and shut-ins, teaching adults, designing and administering church programs, overall parish administration, stimulating parishioners to engage in services to others outside the parish, recruiting new members, organizing and motivating paid staff and volunteers to do the work of the church, presiding at meetings of large groups, teaching children, working with teens.

Are there other areas of competency that you think important for clergy?

In what areas are you most effective? Which tasks do you really enjoy, and why? In what areas are you least effective? How do you manage those areas?

Reviewing the statements on page 66, how would you rate your own professional self-concept? In your life, what influences positively or negatively your response to each of the statements?

What is your perception of your relationship with your bishop and clergy colleagues? How important is that to your own ministry? Why?

Looking at the items which contribute to the overall health of pastors beginning on page 72, are there any surprises or items you might disagree with? How do you fare with each item?

Chapter Six

From your experience, what do you think have been the most significant changes among those ordained in recent years? What is the significance for the church and for clergy?

Do you think that clergy who are women, people of color, single, non-parochial are fully integrated into the life of the diocese? What makes you agree or disagree with this?

If you are one of the faces of clergy described in this chapter, how accepted do you feel in the full life of the diocese? What issues exist as the result of your status? In what specific ways might those issues be addressed, and what can you do to make this happen?

As one of those faces, what do you think is important to your health? What do you do to stay healthy?

Chapter Seven

If you are ordained and married to an ordained person, how has each of you been able to pursue your vocation? What have you found to be the advantages and disadvantages of both of you being ordained? How have you managed to balance your work commitments with time as a family?

What is your view of the appropriate "clergy spouse role"? Do any of the patterns presented beginning on page 103 describe you? Are there other typologies you might add?

What gives you pleasure? What do you like best about being a clergy spouse? What might the problems be? Do you think that the issues are different for a wife than a husband?

What do you think is most important to your health? How do you make that happen?

Chapter Eight

What do you think you need to keep yourself emotionally, spiritually, physically, and vocationally healthy? What might you do for yourself? What steps do you need to take? How might the diocese or judicatory help clergy and spouses stay healthy? How can you help that to happen?

Path Chart I
Predicting Good Overall Health Among Parochial and Non-Parochial Clergy and Spouses

A. CLERGY

Actions

Age (n.s.)	Time spent (0 to 5 plus times per week) Exercising (b = −.09*) Dyadic time with sig. other (b = −.24***) Social time with friends (b = n.s.) Alone time for hobbies (n.s.) Personal prayer/ meditation (b = −.09*)	OVERALL HEALTH (good to poor)

→

R = .31

B. SPOUSES

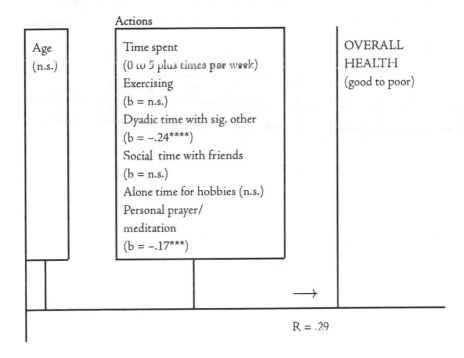

Actions

| Age (n.s.) | Time spent (0 to 5 plus times per week) Exercising (b = n.s.) Dyadic time with sig. other (b = −.24****) Social time with friends (b = n.s.) Alone time for hobbies (n.s.) Personal prayer/ meditation (b = −.17***) | OVERALL HEALTH (good to poor) |

⟶

R = .29

n.s. = not significant

b = beta coefficients. Betas under each of the characteristics charted are the relationship of this characteristic to Overall Health when considering the impact on health of all the characteristics.

* = significance level

   *   .05 to .01

  **   .005 to .001

 ***   .0005 to .0001

****   .under .0001

R = Multiple R. The R's explain how much each additional characteristic helps in predicting health when added to the list in the sequence given.

Path Chart II
Adding Family Degree of Dysfunction to Model for Predicting Good
Overall Health Among Parochial and Non-Parochial Clergy and Spouses

A. CLERGY

Actions

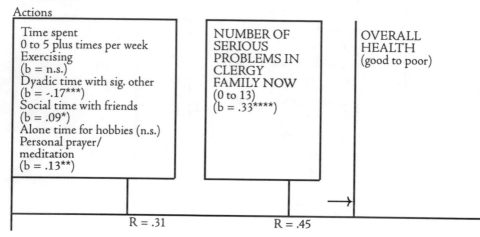

R = .31   R = .45

B. SPOUSES

Actions

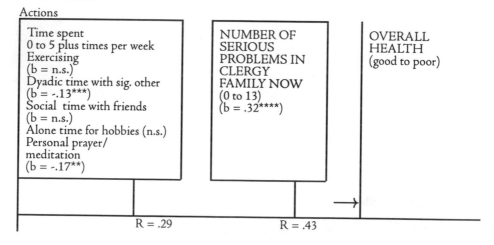

R = .29   R = .43

Path Chart III

Predicting Good Overall Health Among Parochial and Non-Parochial Clergy and Spouses

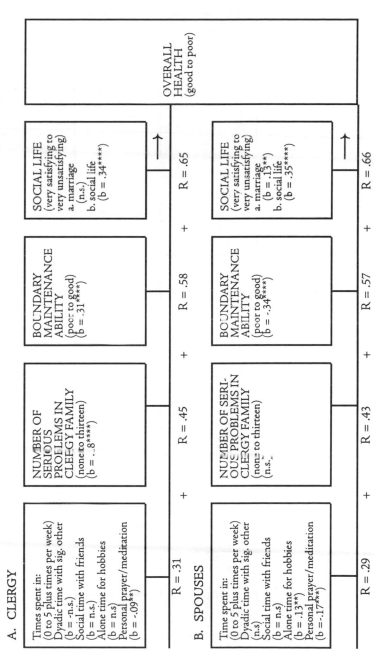

A. CLERGY

Times spent in:
(0 to 5 plus times per week)
Dyadic time with sig. other
(b = -n.s.)
Social time with friends
(b = n.s.)
Alone time for hobbies
(b = n.s)
Personal prayer/meditation
(b = -.09**)

R = .31

+

NUMBER OF SERIOUS PROBLEMS IN CLERGY FAMILY
(none to thirteen)
(b = -.8****)

R = .45

+

BOUNDARY MAINTENANCE ABILITY
(poor to good)
(b = .31****)

R = .58

+

SOCIAL LIFE
(very satisfying to very unsatisfying)
a. marriage
(n.s.)
b. social life
(b = .34****)

R = .65

↑

OVERALL HEALTH
(good to poor)

B. SPOUSES

Time spent in:
(0 to 5 plus times per week)
Dyadic time with sig. other
(n.s)
Social time with friends
(b = n.s)
Alone time for hobbies
(b = .13**)
Personal prayer/meditation
(b = -.17***)

R = .29

+

NUMBER OF SERIOUS PROBLEMS IN CLERGY FAMILY
(none to thirteen)
(n.s.)

R = .43

+

BOUNDARY MAINTENANCE ABILITY
(poor to good)
(b = -.34****)

R = .57

+

SOCIAL LIFE
(very satisfying to very unsatisfying)
a. marriage
(b = .13**)
b. social life
(b = .35****)

R = .66

↑

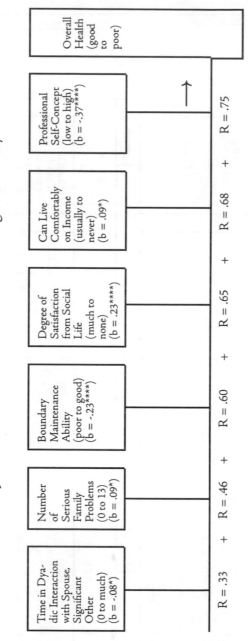

Path Chart IV

Major Predictors of Good Overall Health Among Pastors Only

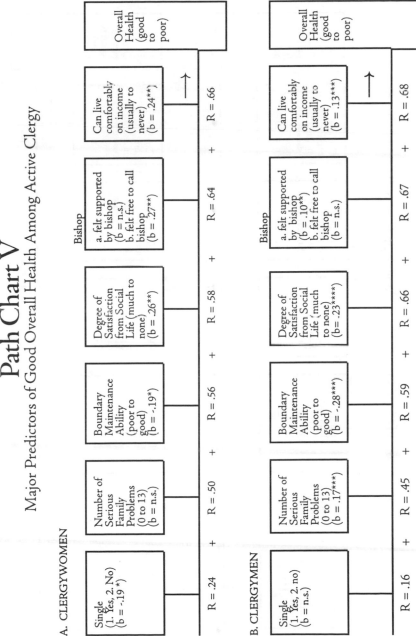

Path Chart V
Major Predictors of Good Overall Health Among Active Clergy

Path Chart VI

Major Predictors of Good Overall health Among Spouses of Parochial Clergy

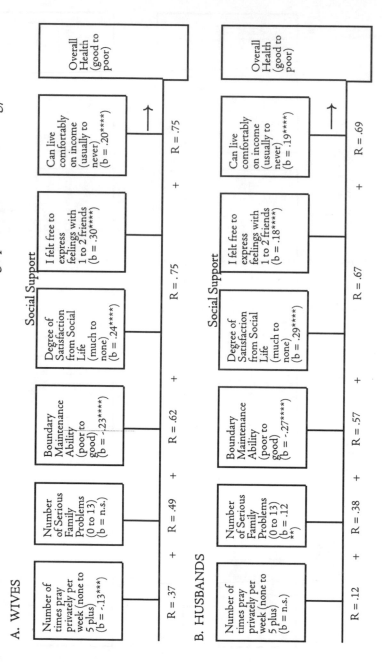

Bibliography

Books

Bondi, Roberta C., *To Pray and to Love: Conversations on Prayer with the Early Church*. Minneapolis: Fortress Press, 1991.

Carroll, Jackson W., *As One with Authority*. Louisville: Westminster/John Knox Press, 1991.

Carroll, Jackson W., Barbara I Iargrove, and Adair T. Lummis, *Women of the Cloth: A New Opportunity for Churches*. San Francisco: Harper and Row, 1983.

Covell, Jr., David R., *Who Do Men Say That I Am?* Strategic Research Services Group, Executive Council of the Episcopal Church, New York: Episcopal Church Center, 1970.

Deming, Laura, and Jack Stubbs, *Men Married to Ministers*. Washington: Alban Institute, 1986.

Douglas, William, *Ministers' Wives*. New York: Harper and Row, 1965.

Friedman, Edwin H., *Generation to Generation: Family Process in Church and Synagogue*. New York: Guilford Press, 1985.

Fukuyama, Yoshio, *The Ministry in Transition*. University Park, Pa.: The Penn State University Press, 1972.

Gilbert, Barbara G., *Who Ministers to Ministers? A Study of Support Systems for Clergy and Spouses*. Washington: Alban Institute, 1987.

Glasse, James D., *Profession: Minister*. Nashville: Abingdon Press, 1968.

Greenbacker, Liz, and Sherry Taylor, *Private Lives of Ministers' Wives*. Far Hills, N.J.: New Horizons Press, 1991.

Hadden, Jeffrey K., *The Gathering Storm in Churches*. Garden City, N.Y.: Doubleday, 1969.

Holmes III, Urban T., *The Priest in Community: Exploring the Roots of Ministry*. New York: Seabury Press, 1978.

Jacquet, Jr., Constant, *Women Ministers in 1986 and 1977: a Ten Year View*. New York: National Council of Churches, 1988.

Jencks, Christopher, and David Riesman, *The Academic Revolution*. Garden City, N.Y.: Doubleday, 1968.

Jud, Gerald J., Edgar W. Mills, Jr., and Genevieve Walters Burch, *Ex-Pastors: Why Men Leave the Parish Ministry*. Philadelphia: Pilgrim Press, 1970.

Kerr, Michael E., and Murray Bowen, *Family Evaluation*. New York: W. W. Norton, 1988.

Lebacqz, Karen, and Ronald Burton, *Sex in the Parish*. Louisville: Westminster/John Knox Press, 1991.

Lee, Cameron, and Jack Balswick, *Life in a Glass House: The Minister's Family in Its Unique Social Context*. Grand Rapids, Mich.: Ministry Resources Library, Zondervan Publishing House, 1989.

Mace, David, and Vera Mace, *What's Happening to Clergy Marriages*. Nashville: Abingdon Press, 1980.

Majka, Linda, *Sexual Harassment in the United Methodist Church*. Dayton, Ohio: General Council on Ministries, United Methodist Church, 1990.

Maloney, H. Newton, and Richard A. Hunt, *The Psychology of Clergy*. Harrisburg, Pa.: Morehouse Publishing, 1991.

Mead, Loren B., Barry Evans, Edgar W. Mills, Jr., and Clement W. Welsh, *Personal and Professional Needs of the Clergy of the Episcopal Church*. New York: The Episcopal Church Foundation, 1988.

Menninger, Karl, *The Vital Balance: The Life Process in Mental Health and Illness*. New York: The Viking Press, 1963.

Mickey, Paul, and Ginny W. Ashmore, *Clergy Families: Is Normal Life Possible?* Grand Rapids, Mich.: Zondervan Publishing House, 1991.

Nouwen, Henri J. M., *The Wounded Healer*. New York: Image Book, Doubleday, 1979.

Rallings, E. M., and David J. Pratto, *Two-Clergy Marriages: A Special Case of Dual Careers*. Lantham, Md.: University Press of America, 1984.

Retiger, Lloyd, *Coping with Clergy Burnout*. Valley Forge, Pa.: Judson Press, 1981.

Ridley, Jasper, *Thomas Cranmer*. Oxford: Clarendon Press, 1962.

Roof, Wade Clark, and William McKinney, *American Mainline Religion: Its Changing Shape and Future*. New Brunswick, N.J.: Rutgers University Press, 1987.

Smith, Donald P., *Clergy in the Crossfire*. Philadelphia: The Westminster Press, 1972.

Stewart, Charles William, *Person and Profession: Career Development in Ministry*. Nashville: Abingdon Press, 1974.

Zikmund, Barbara Brown, Adair T. Lummis, and Patricia M. Y. Chang, *An Uphill Calling: Ordained Women and Men in the Contemporary Protestant Church*. Louisville: Westminister/John Knox Press, 1997.

Articles and papers cited

Barstow, Anne Llewellyn, "The First Generations of Anglican Clergy Wives: Heroines or Whores?" *Historical Magazine of the Protestant Episcopal Church*. March 1983.

Episcopal Life. Series "Clergy Sexual Abuse" starting in the September 1991 issue.

Hughes, Everett, and A. DeBaggis, "Systems of Theological Education in the United States." E. Hughes et al., *Education for the Professions of Medicine, Law, Theology and Social Welfare.* New York: Carnegie Commission, 1973.

Judson, George, "Congregation Confronts a Changing Ministry." *The New York Times*, July 19–20, 1992.

Kadushin, Charles, "The Professional Self-Concept of Music Students." *American Journal of Sociology*, Vol. 75, 1969.

Larsen, Ellis, and James M. Shopshire, "A Profile of Contemporary Seminarians." Entire issue of *Theological Education*, Vol. 24, Spring 1988.

Lummis, Adair T., "Minister, Debtor and Mother." Paper read at the Society for the Scientific Study of Religion—Religious Research Association (SSSR-RRA) annual meetings. Louisville, October 1987.

Maeder, Thomas, "Wounded Healers," *The Atlantic Monthly*, January 1989.

Marciano, Teresa, "Corporate Church, Ministry and Ministerial Family: Embedded Employment and Measures of Success." *Marriage and Family Review*, Vol. 15: 171–193, 1990.

Menninger Perspective, No. 4, 1988. Quarterly of the Menninger Foundation, Topeka.

Mills, Jr., Edgar W., "Review of Recent Social Science Research on Stress." Mead, Loren B., Barry Evans, Edgar W. Mills, Jr., and Clement W. Welsh, *Personal and Professional Needs of the Clergy of the Episcopal Church.* New York: The Episcopal Church Foundation, 1988.

Nesbitt, Paula D., "Clergy Feminization: Controlled Labor or Liberationist Change?" Paper presented at the annual meetings of the Association for the Sociology of Religion. Cincinnati, August 1991.

Nesbitt, Paula D., "Lamentations: The Politics of Gender and Ministry." Paper delivered at the Society for the Scientific Study of Religion. Washington, November 1992.

Norell, Elizabeth J., "Clergy Family Satisfaction: A Review." *Family Science Review*, Vol. 4: 69–93, 1989.

Nouwen, Henri J. M., "Reborn from Above," *Spiritual Life*, Spring 1992. Quarterly of the Washington Province of Discalced Carmelite Friars, Inc., Washington.

Richmond, Lee, Carole Rayburn, and Lynn Roger, "Clergymen, Clergywomen and Their Spouses: Stress in Professional Religious Families." *Journal of Career Development*, Vol. 12. 01 85, September 1985.

Thielens, Wagner, "The Occupational Self-Image of the Law Student." Paper read at the American Sociological Association national meetings, 1963.

Turner, Franklin D., and Adair T. Lummis, "Black Clergy in the Episcopal Church: Recruitment, Training, and Deployment." Report produced by the Office for Black Ministries, Episcopal Church Center, New York, 1979.

Warner, Janelle, and John D. Carter "Loneliness, Marital Adjustment and Burnout in Pastoral and Lay Persons." *Journal of Psychology and Theology*, Vol. 12: 125–131, 1984.

Whittemore, Hank, "Ministers Under Stress," *Parade Magazine*, April 14, 1991: 20–21.

Wortman, Julie A., "High Hurdles Confront Those Seeking Ordination," *Episcopal Life*, September 1991.

About the Authors

ADAIR T. LUMMIS is a sociologist with a doctorate from Columbia University. She is a Research Faculty Associate at the Center for Social and Religious Research at Hartford Seminary, Hartford, Conn. In addition to working on the Clergy Family Project for the past decade, she has been principal researcher on over fifteen studies for organizations within the Episcopal Church. These include studies on the permanent diaconate, black Episcopal clergy, Episcopal clergy housing, funding for the national church, the full participation of Episcopal lay and clergy women in congregations and dioceses across the United States, clergywomen of Province I, Episcopal bishops, spouses of Episcopal bishops, Episcopal theological education and seminaries, the Episcopal Health and Vocational Inventory, and, most recently, spiritually vital Episcopal congregations.

Adair Lummis is co-author of two multi-denominational studies, *Women of the Cloth* (1983) and *Defecting in Place* (1993). A third study, *An Uphill Calling,* is forthcoming in 1997.

She has two daughters and one grandson.

ROBERTA CHAPIN WALMSLEY began her career as a musician, with her undergraduate degree from Washington University. She studied piano with Leo Miller and organ with Benjamin Harrison and Robert Glasgow. Following marriage and a move to the East Coast, she became actively involved with children's issues in Brooklyn, N.Y., and, when her own two children reached school age, with desegregation efforts in the New York City school system. This eventually led to a Masters in Social Work from the University of Connecticut and work with families of children in special education in a school system in that state. Ten years ago she was asked to be a coordinator of the Clergy Family Project, a program undertaken by the Episcopal Family Network. She was responsible for the development of the *Manual for Clergy Family Project Committees*, a process for helping dioceses develop support systems for clergy and clergy families. She retired as coordinator of the project in 1996.

Roberta Walmsley has written and spoken on issues of health and wellness in clergy families. She presently works with advocacy groups for children and women in New Hampshire, to which she moved with her husband, Bishop Arthur Walmsley, on his retirement from the Diocese of Connecticut.